OUT OF THE MAZE

THE TRUE STORY OF THE BIGGEST JAILBREAK IN EUROPE SINCE THE SECOND WORLD WAR

DEREK DUNNE

GILL AND MACMILLAN
DUBLIN

Published in Ireland by
Gill and Macmillan Ltd
Goldenbridge
Dublin 8
with associated companies in
Auckland, Delhi, Gaborone, Hamburg, Harare,
Hong Kong, Johannesburg, Kuala Lumpur, Lagos, London,
Manzini, Melbourne, Mexico City, Nairobi,
New York, Singapore, Tokyo
© Derek Dunne 1988
Print origination in Ireland by
Graphic Plan
Printed in the United Kingdom by
Richard Clay Ltd, Bungay, Suffolk

British Library Cataloguing in Publication Data

Dunne, Derek, 1956 —
    Out of the Maze.
    1. Lisburn. Prisons. Maze Prisons.
    Prisoners. Organised mass escapes,
    1983
    I. title
    365'.641

ISBN 0-7171-1607-7

Contents

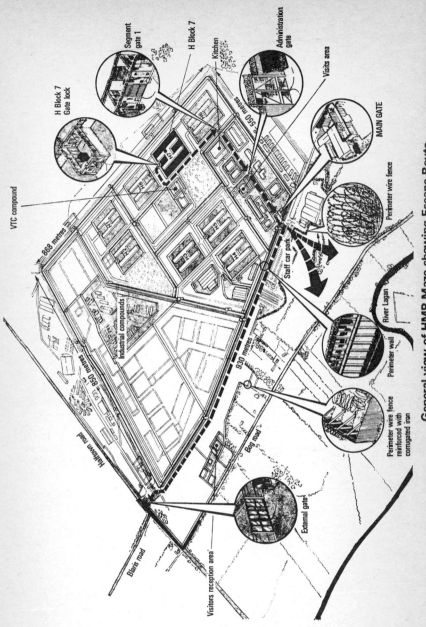

General view of HMP Maze showing Escape Route

Segment gate 1

H Block 7

Kitchen

H Block 7 Gate lock

Administration gate

Visits area

VTC compound

MAIN GATE

Perimeter wire fence

868 metres

Industrial compounds

Staff car park

River Lagan

Perimeter wall

930 metres

830 metres

Halftown road

Bog road

Perimeter wire fence reinforced with corrugated iron

Blaris road

Visitors reception area

External gate

550 metres

Preface

This is the inside story of how the Maze prison escape of September 1983 took place. The account is based on interviews with those who planned and executed the escape, some of whom are still on the run, some of whom are in prison and others who have since been released. Where prison officers are mentioned by name, descriptions of their actions are taken from evidence given to the police following the escape and evidence given to the courts. The same applies to British soldiers, RUC constables and RUC reservists. The takeover of H-Block 7 is based on interviews with those who took part, on evidence given by prison officers to the police and on the Hennessy Report commissioned in the wake of the escape.

The jail is officially known as HM Prison, The Maze. Republicans still call it by its original name—Long Kesh. Sometimes it is referred to as H-Blocks, or just the Blocks. Where it is relevant and depending on the point of view of the narrative, I have referred to the prison by various names. The escape was the largest in Europe since the Second World War, from one of Europe's most secure prisons.

I am indebted to all those who helped in the preparation of this book. Dozens of people were interviewed. For obvious reasons they do not wish to be named.

Derek Dunne
Dublin
May 1988

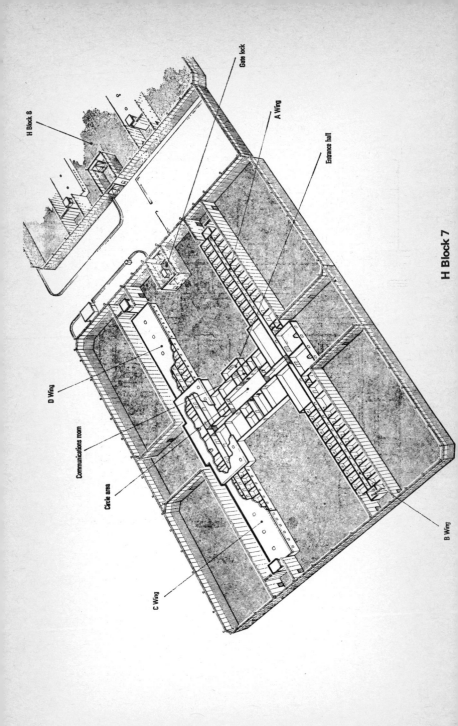

H Block 7

H Block 8

Gate lock

A Wing

Entrance hall

D Wing

Communications room

Circle area

C Wing

B Wing

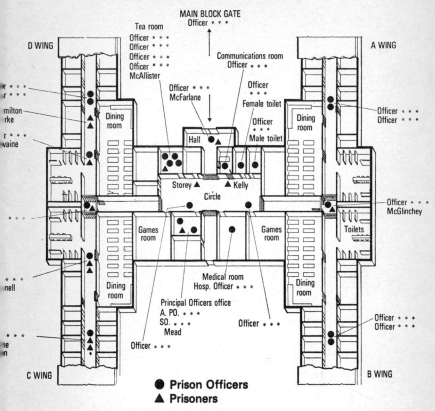

MAIN BLOCK GATE
Officer * * *

Tea room
Officer * * *
Officer * * *
Officer * * *
Officer * * *
McAllister

Communications room
Officer * * *

D WING

A WING

Officer * * *
r * * *

milton
rke

r * * *
vaine

Officer * * *
McFarlane

Officer
* * *
Female toilet

Officer
* * *
Male toilet

Officer * * *
Officer * * *

Dining
room

Dining
room

Hall

Storey ▲   ▲ Kelly

Circle

* * *

Games
room

Games
room

Officer * * *
McGlinchey

Toilets

nell

Dining
room

Medical room
Hosp. Officer * * *

Dining
room

Principal Officers office
A. PO. * * *
SO.   * * *
Mead

Officer * * *

Officer * * *
Officer * * *

* * *
he
n

Officer * * *

C WING

B WING

● **Prison Officers**
▲ **Prisoners**

The Circle area of H Block 7 at the time of the takeover

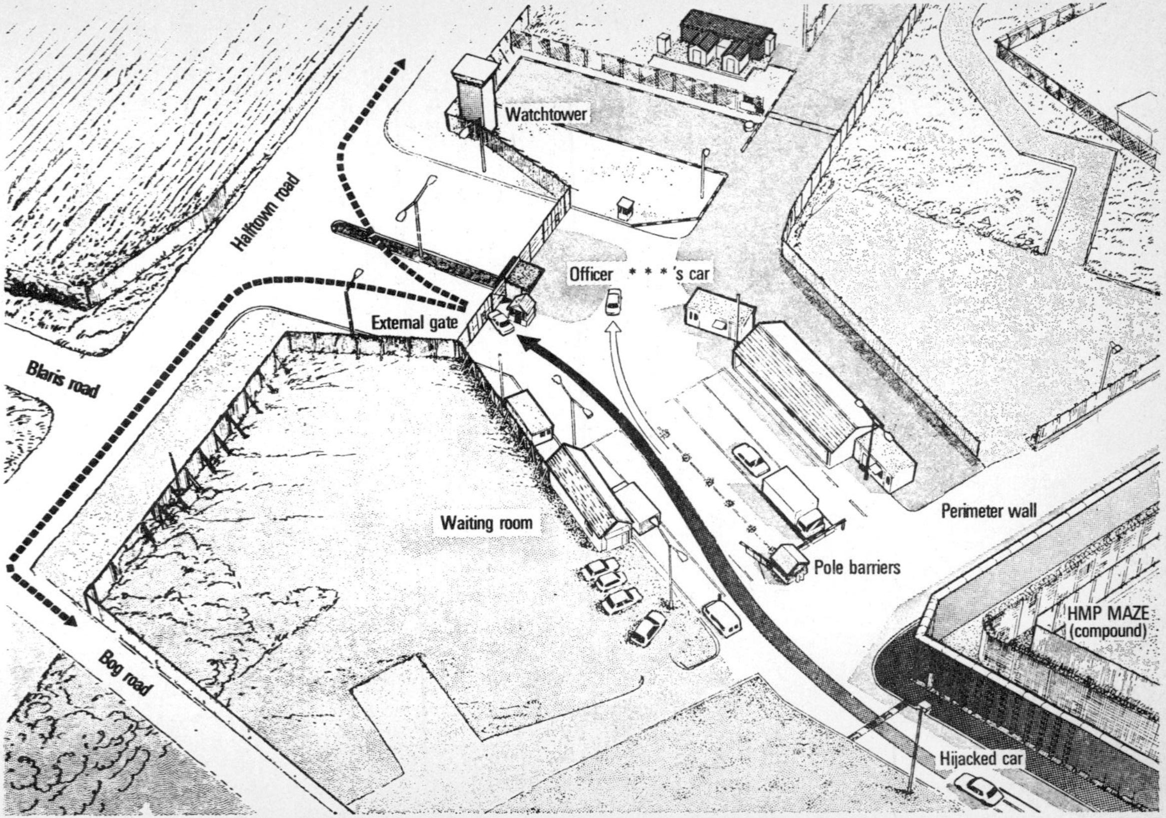
Watchtower
Halftown road
Officer * * * 's car
External gate
Blaris road
Waiting room
Perimeter wall
Pole barriers
HMP MAZE
(compound)
Bog road
Hijacked car

The External Gate

Prologue

The Block was going to be a doddle to take if the plans were anything to go by. The Block would be no problem. It was after that the problems started. Just around 2.30 pm on that Sunday the Provos had five lifers working in the Circle. First of all there was Bobby Storey, known to the men as Big Bob. Then there was Brendan 'Bik' McFarlane, and Gerry Kelly, and Tony McAllister and Brendan Mead. The Circle based in the centre of H-Block 7 was really a rectangle and they had it covered. The five men would be able to take control there. Each of the five men had a shortarm, though one weapon was a replica since there had been problems with the weapons at the last minute. All the warders were being watched, and the men were waiting for the signal to go. When the bumper was called for, that would be the signal. The bumper was a cleaning machine and when that was called for they would have to move fast and watch the warders and the alarms. They would have to watch some of their own men who had no idea what was about to happen.

George Smylie was second in command of H-Block 7 that day. He was standing outside his office in the Circle not doing anything much. Brendan Mead walked over to him. Mead said he had a problem and he wanted to talk to Smylie about it. Could he talk about it in the office? It was a personal problem? No problem. Smylie opened the door to the office and led the way in. Acting Principal Officer Robert George was sitting in there behind his desk and he paid little attention to the two men. It wasn't unusual to see prisoners coming in lately with their problems. Things had been pretty quiet on H7 for a good few months now. Mead started to tell his story—there were a few of the lads giving him hassle on the Block and he wasn't too sure what he should do about it. He said he had thought about

1

moving to another Block but he wondered aloud if that was the right thing to do. Smylie was an understanding man. This sort of thing happened all the time. People moved from Block to Block because of the hassle.

In the Circle the other four men were moving into position. There were 125 prisoners in the Block in all and many of them did not know what was happening. Less than half had any idea at all. The Communications Room was the security nerve centre of the Circle and the entire Block. There were alarm buttons and double doors and telephones in there. There was a heap of trouble there if anything went wrong. Gerry Kelly moved towards the Communications Room pushing the bumper. And then there was the Officers Mess just off the Circle—more trouble. Tony McAllister moved towards the Mess. It needed to be cleaned and McAllister as orderly needed a hand. Bobby Storey was there—the right man in the right place at the right time. It was convenient. Bobby said he would give him a hand. There were four warders drinking tea in the Mess as the two prisoners moved closer. Then Gerry Kelly came back with the bumper and he could see Rab Kerr and Sean McGlinchey. They were both in the grilles in opposite ends of the Block. Both were between two gates which gave access to two wings each. Brendan McFarlane had by now moved towards the Hall area which gave access to the entire Block. The signal came.

Back in Smylie's office Mead produced a gun. Everybody had to hit the deck. Now everybody in the Circle had to move at once.

Of the 125 prisoners in H7 that day, forty-four were in for murder or conspiracy to murder, forty-one were in for possession or use of explosives, twenty-eight were in for possession or use of weapons. Twenty-four were serving life with little or no chance of seeing freedom before the next century. Eighty-eight were serving more than ten years and nearly all were in their twenties. After more than a year's work, the Provos had engineered a situation whereby they had exactly who they wanted in the Block that day.

Within ten seconds of Mead producing his weapon in Smylie's office the Provos would have to take total control of the Block. Within ninety minutes thirty-eight of them would have to drive through several gates and out of the prison undetected by the authorities. If they succeeded, it would be the largest jail break in Western Europe since the Second World War and the

2

culmination of two years' solid work. It would also be the largest operation the Provos ever carried out, involving more than 140 men and women at least. The impact the escapees could have on the IRA on the outside was incalculable. But the curious fact was that the man who had dreamed up the entire escape and who had planned it down to the last detail was not going on it. He wasn't even in the same Block. But around the time that Mead produced his weapon he was sweating.

1

Long Kesh

They called him Papillon. Or sometimes, the Wee Devil. He had never stopped trying to get out, not in ten years. His story mirrored the recent history of the North, its troubles and its prisons.

Papillon had got involved with the IRA in Ardoyne early on. It was hard not to get involved then. The issues were clear cut. There was a need to defend communities. Somebody had to do it and the IRA looked the best bet in those early days. Ardoyne, a small Catholic enclave in North Belfast surrounded on all sides by Protestants, was a particularly sensitive area. In the early seventies it was easier to die than to live there. In 1973 Papillon was caught for armed robbery. He was on remand for a few weeks and tried to escape twice. The first time he dressed up as a warder and tried to get away. He was caught by a warder who went on to become a governor. Papillon got on well with him. There were no hard feelings—almost. The second time he tried to get out was when he thought up the idea of running a rope from D Wing in Crumlin Road Jail across to the nearby hospital. He would get across the wall from there. The plan fell through, so Papillon went to court and got seven years for the robbery. He arrived in the Cages in Long Kesh, then starting to fill up with the young men of the North. He took the view that the only way to continue the fight in jail was to escape. Papillon, the man with the brass neck, spent his days dreaming up new ways around the old problems. The old problems were the walls and the wire and the sentries and how to get away. He perfected his carving ability; he was good at woodwork and was especially good at carving replica weapons, handy for an escape attempt. He played a small bit of guitar, and like others who play a musical instrument he was very popular.

One of his earlier attempts at getting away presented itself to him on a plate. He noticed a new warder on the gate, a greenhorn. And there was a small kitten in the Cages. Papillon took the kitten, and holding it gently to his breast, walked to the gate and told the new warder that part of his duty was to report to the doctor with the sick kitten at least once a day. He managed to get as far as the prison hospital before he was caught. He schemed day and night to get out. There was the famous British Army Patrol, for example. This was in 1975. With a load of other prisoners, they dressed up as British soldiers, and started to patrol around the camp. They almost got away. They were coming up to a small wicket gate which would take them out of the camp when they were challenged by real British soldiers. They were all charged with attempted escape and were brought to Newry Courthouse. There were ten of them there in the cells, waiting to be brought up to face the court. They were messing about with the grille on the windows when somebody noticed it was loose. It took them a matter of a few moments to scramble out. Papillon was free again. He went back to the IRA, back to the war. By now, he was married and with three small sons, aged four, five and eight. He continued to remain on active service with the IRA. He was thirty years old.

He didn't crop up for some time after that, until March of the following year. It was early on a Sunday morning when he was part of a six-man IRA unit heading down the New Lodge Road in Belfast in the van. They were carrying what amounted to an arsenal—two bombs and five shortarms. On the way to carry out a bombing they were stopped at the bottom of the road by a British Army patrol. There were five soldiers altogether, but only two of them were on the road, the remaining three preferring to stay inside the jeep. A soldier recognised Tony Hughes from Ardoyne straight away. Bootser, as he was known, had long flowing ginger hair. One of the soldiers started to search the van, while the second took names and addresses. The six IRA men poured onto the road. Then the soldier taking down the names made a mistake—he faced up the New Lodge. Bootser hit him for all he was worth and all six men scattered in different directions. Papillon was picked up on the M1 motorway the following year; he was a pillion passenger on a motorbike at the time. He got ten years. He was back in the Cages of Long Kesh again, and his wife gave birth to twins shortly afterwards.

The Cages of Long Kesh were special at the time. The men had political status and were treated like prisoners of war. The IRA had its own structures, camp commandants and routines. The men trained and drilled. They lived in Nissan huts. Their major preoccupation was trying to escape. Indeed, as prisoners of war the IRA men were duty bound to try and escape and rejoin the fight on the outside.

Papillon, small and stocky, held classes in the huts. He liked to laugh and tell jokes a lot. Constantly with a smile on his face, he stood in front of a class with a blackboard and outlined what they knew about the camp. The scene was straight out of *The Great Escape*. How much they knew about the camp was covered, how much they needed to know and how they could get that information. Getting the information they didn't possess meant the difference between a successful escape and getting caught. Meanwhile, he had some plans of his own about getting away.

He dressed up as a civilian warder. Civilian warders were charged with maintaining the camp. Papillon decided that he could get away by fixing some lights. So he dressed up in overalls, got a ladder, and cut his way through the first wire. He got 700 yards down the road. He was repairing another light near the fence when he was caught. He had decided to go at lunch time, but alas, civilian warders were not renowned for their over-enthusiasm for working their lunch hour, and he was caught again. Curiously, he remained in the Cages, despite the fact that he should have been moved across the way to the Blocks. The H-Blocks had been newly constructed, and there was no political status. After 1976 anybody convicted was denied political status, and anybody caught escaping was deemed to have left the Cages voluntarily, and lost the status. When he failed in this attempt, two other men decided to make their way to Papillon's Cage—11—and pool their resources. Brendan McFarlane and Pat McGeown arrived in Cage 11. The escape classes went on.

Papillon thought the best way out of the Camp was to dig tunnels. The soft sandy ground of the camp was ideal for digging. The prison authorities were aware of these plans and, week after week, they closed off the new tunnels they discovered. But Papillon had a gift—he could convince people he had the best plan in the world for escaping. And every day, he stayed in front of his blackboard for at least an hour. In those classes, he

6

exercised another gift he had; he brought people with different skills together. Then another plan was hatched.

There was one prisoner who was good at carving weapons. Papillon wasn't too bad at it himself, so they made replica weapons. They got another prisoner who was good at scrounging to get them some more materials—three pairs of blue trousers and some anoraks. They had collected fireman's and busman's buttons which were handy for sewing onto the cut-down-to-size anoraks. But the difficult part was making prison warders' hats. They had all the rest. There had been a tailor in the Camp, but he was long released. Before that, Papillon had picked his brains. He learned how to make the peaked caps, as well as the uniforms. He cut the bottom out of a steel basin and cut a two-inch rim. That served as the basis for the hat. Cardboard painted black with a piece of plastic would serve as a peak. Papillon and McFarlane and McGeown had held onto prison warders' cap badges during a riot at the Camp earlier in the year. You never knew when something like that could come in handy. So the three were ready to leave. They had checked out the exit. Warders were let out of the camp once they had discs with numbers on them. These would get the three men out of the gate; they would then separate, and meet up later in a pre-arranged place.

It was just 3.30 pm on the last day of March 1978 when the three made their way towards the gate. There were only one or two warders about as they headed for the hut near the exit. They planned to take a warder's car for the getaway. But just before they got to the gate, they discovered that the passes had been changed. All they knew was that discs were no longer being used, it seemed as if warders were handing in plastic cards now. Vans and cars were moving in and out and then McFarlane made a mistake. He went to the blind side of one of the vans. A warder passed him by, recognised him and said nothing. The three managed to get out. They were caught almost at once.

They were deemed to have left the Cages voluntarily, to have given up their political status voluntarily. They were transferred across the way to the new H-Blocks. When they were moved, they refused to do prison work, they considered they were political prisoners and refused to be criminalised. When they refused to work, they were locked in their cells. They went on the blanket, which meant that they wore no clothes. They were

7

caught up in an escalating protest. Eventually the men on protest would become human armalites. Protest by starvation would develop into protest by death. There was a world of difference between the Cages and H-Blocks, even though they were side by side. Over the next couple of years, the battle-ground would switch to the prisons, and especially to Long Kesh.

Long Kesh was built on the site of an old World War Two airfield, about eight miles from Belfast. It was originally a compound of unheated Nissan huts, barbed wire, floodlights and watch towers with British soldiers. In August 1971, when internment without trial was introduced, most of the internees found their way here. Later, more Cages were opened to house separately convicted republican and loyalist prisoners.

The North started off the seventies with three prisons holding about 600 prisoners, but the prison population increased fourfold in the following years. The increases were due to men and women convicted of offences which were politically motivated, and which aimed to topple a State which was seen and generally acknowledged to be discriminatory against the minority Catholic population.

Long Kesh was run pretty much along the lines of any prisoner-of-war camp. The image of Long Kesh as promoted around the world in the early seventies was not lost on the Prime Minister of Northern Ireland, Brian Faulkner. He noted that the prison 'came to look like the prisoner-of-war camps with which the post-war generation were all too familiar. In the autumn [1971] it became the main detention centre for terrorist suspects, and the IRA propaganda machine sent pictures of the watch towers, patrolling soldiers and wire fences around the world to reinforce their claims that an oppressive military regime was being operated in Ulster.'

The men in Long Kesh were organised and disciplined according to strict military structures. They drilled with dummy wooden guns, carved from wood supplied by the prison authorities. They held lectures on revolutionary politics, revolutionary warfare and how to get out of the prison. The IRA men in Long Kesh became the Fourth Battalion of the IRA's Belfast Brigade, after the other three based in the city. They came under the control of the Brigade Staff, which ultimately was under the Control of the seven-person IRA Army Council. The changing nature of that relationship between the Fourth Brigade and the Army Council was to have very significant repercussions in the years ahead.

By the middle of 1972 it was clear that the riots and resistance across the North were not going to disappear just because internment had been introduced. Internment had the opposite effect and violence escalated. In June 1972 Belfast IRA man Billy McKee, who was convicted for an arms offence, went on hunger strike demanding political status for sentenced prisoners, the kind of status enjoyed by the internees. The IRA had always used the hunger-strike weapon as a weapon of last resort and they had a good record in using it. They generally got their way. Rioting broke out following rumours of McKee's death. He was quite alive, but the British conceded what amounted to political status in settling the dispute. The concessions, granted as of right to republican prisoners, were the right to visits and parcels, the right for prisoners to wear their own clothes, the right of prisoners to associate freely, the right of prisoners not to do prison work, and segregation from loyalist prisoners. The settlement sowed the seeds of battle further up the road.

In 1975 it began to sink in that the IRA weren't going away. A British think-tank, comprising people from the Army, police and MI5 came up with a new policy. It involved 'normalisation', 'criminalisation' and 'Ulsterisation'. The IRA were a law-and-order problem, not a political threat. The local RUC would be used to deal with them. The IRA would be processed through the courts—albeit non-jury, special courts—and would be treated the same way as ordinary criminals. Lord Gardiner noted that the compound system at Long Kesh was most unsatisfactory. The men were doing as they pleased. They went about thinking that they might get an amnesty. This expectation was not unreasonable considering the fact that the British government had held face-to-face talks with the IRA in 1972 and, three years later, entered into a unilateral ceasefire and communicated with republicans through newly-established 'truce incident centres'. The British now decided that it was time to stop all this foolish thinking, and stated their intention to phase out political status on 1 March 1976. They sweetened the deal by increasing remission to fifty per cent for conforming prisoners. This applied to prisoners in the North of Ireland and not to those in the rest of the United Kingdom. There would be no special deals or privileges for men convicted after that date. However, special courts, special laws, special police forces and special measures were still in force. There were also special prisons. And with the new policy came a new prison.

It was built beside the Cages at Long Kesh. The new prison was renamed 'Her Majesty's Prison, The Maze'. It was an attempt to get away from the image that had built up around Long Kesh as a prisoner-of-war camp. But the new name never really caught on. People still called it Long Kesh. Republicans called it the H-Blocks, or just the Blocks. Men convicted after the magic cut-off date were to be sent to the new prison. Men convicted prior to that date were to retain their political status and stay in the Cages, still drilling away and dreaming of amnesties and new ways to escape. The entire compound was surrounded with a seventeen-foot-high concrete wall which was two miles long. The wall was overlooked by a dozen sentry boxes, and armed British soldiers took up residence in them. The new prison was called The Maze (Cellular) as distinct from The Maze (Compound), where the Cages were located.

It was the most luxurious prison in Western Europe, according to the British authorities. There were eight single storey grey Blocks, each in the shape of an H. They cost about a million pounds sterling each. Each arm of the H was defined as a Wing and held twenty-five cells. The idea was that one person would be accommodated per cell, but two could easily fit. Each Block also had a dining-room, exercise yard and hobbies room. The centre 'bar' of the H was known as the Circle. The Circle was really a rectangle, and held the classrooms, offices for the warders, a medical treatment room and stores. There were further facilities outside the Blocks themselves. These included workshops, a hospital with a dental surgery, an indoor sports hall, snooker and basketball facilities, two all-weather sports pitches. Vocational training in everything from vehicle maintenance to horticulture was provided. And there were classes in everything from music to Irish. People might be forgiven for thinking that the place sounded like a holiday camp from the description. But prison is still prison no matter how comfortable it appears to be.

In 1975, before the first men moved into the new prison, the *Sunday Times* newspaper revealed that files on visitors to republican prisoners at Long Kesh were being passed on to loyalist paramilitaries by sympathetic members of the RUC and UDR. Naturally enough, this promoted a siege mentality within republican circles. It was the end of that year before the last of the internees were released. But what republicans called the 'conveyor belt' system of justice had already started. This involved arrest under special laws and detention for seven days, often culminating in allegations of brutality and charges based solely on self-incriminating statements or 'confessions'. Bail was denied and effective internment through remand could last for years. Then the case was heard before a juryless, single-judge court. The final destination was Long Kesh, the H-Blocks, The Maze. The idea grew that once you were arrested, there was no way off that belt. And the belt began to deliver more men and women in greater numbers into the prison system in the North.

The Blocks were designed to control the men by restricting their movement. But what was not envisaged was that the men might be prisoners by constraint, but that their consent was also needed if the prison was to run smoothly. In 1976 the IRA declared its intention to fight the new criminalisation process. 'We are prepared to die for the right to political status', they said, 'and those who try to take it away from us must be fully prepared to pay the same price.' The British government insisted that Northern Ireland's troubles was a law-and-order issue. The IRA said it was a war. Five bitter years followed.

Ciaran Nugent was the first man on the blanket in September 1976. He refused to wear prison clothes and was locked into his cell twenty-four hours a day. So he wore a blanket and automatically lost fifty per cent remission for refusing to conform. His sentence was doubled. He lost three privileged visits and one statutory visit every month. The path he took was followed by hundreds of others in the months and years which followed. Inevitably there was confrontation with the warders. The cells were seven-foot by eight-foot concrete boxes, containing nothing but a mattress, three blankets, a bible and a cell mate. After a while the prisoners donned the prison clothes to take one visit a month and establish communications with the IRA on the outside. They submitted to the degrading mirror search. This involved squatting over a mirror and having the warders poking around your back passage to see if there was anything up there. That went on for a couple of years and then the protest escalated

11

again. Prisoners were allowed to wash wearing only a towel. The prison authorities refused the men a second towel to dry themselves. On the basis that they were not going to be made to walk around naked, they refused to come out of their cells. The no-wash protest was up and running. The men used chamber pots to go to the toilet. Then there was further escalation.

The situation was getting more tense by the week, with inevitable confrontation between warders and prisoners. According to the prisoners the warders started to throw the contents of the chamber pots back through the doors of the cells. Then the dirty protest started. This involved smearing the faeces on the walls to diffuse the smell, and pouring urine out through the cracks in the doors. Then the prison authorities tried to break the prisoners; there were forced washes, inevitable fights, beatings, accusations of intimidation. There were attempts at humiliation on a massive scale. Not all incoming prisoners joined the protest. Some conformed. The republican camp within the jail, made up largely of IRA followers but some from the INLA, was split.

In 1978 Cardinal O'Fiaich visited the Blocks and talked with some of the men on protest. What he had to say when he came out was embarrassing to the prison authorities and a damning indictment of what he found. 'One could hardly allow an animal to remain in such conditions, let alone a human being. The nearest approach I have seen to it...was the slums of Calcutta. The stench and filth in some of the cells with the remains of rotten food and human excreta scattered around the walls was almost unbearable.' And then in January 1979 the prison authorities made one of their biggest mistakes.

They took all the leading IRA men and put them in the same Block: H6. There were thirty-two of them, and they included Papillon, Brendan McFarlane, Pat McGeown, Brendan Hughes, Bobby Sands, Sid Walsh. They started what amounted to an IRA officers' training academy. Political debate and discussion followed—the role of guerrilla warfare, the strengths and weaknesses of the IRA campaign, armed propaganda, other struggles. Through debate the men came to the view, for example, that just because people were in armed resistance, it didn't make it right or justified. They stayed there for nine months before they were dispersed throughout the Blocks. By then they had designed structures for training prisoners and they had the basics in the techniques of resistance. There were by now 1,365 men in the Blocks, 837 republicans and 341 loyalists—the balance was made up of 'ordinary criminals'. The battle was being waged inside and outside the prison. Prisoners were coming under pressure from the warders, the name of the warders would be sent to the IRA on the outside, the warder would be shot dead. The killing would provoke other warders to take it out on the prisoners on the inside. It was a vicious circle. Eighteen prison officers were killed, including one woman warder. Towards the end of 1980 it was decided that a hunger strike was the only way to settle the matter once and for all. The strike would generate sympathetic public opinion which could be galvanised into positive action. Hunger striking was the old weapon of republicans and one which had not let them down in the past.

'The Government cannot concede on the principle that is at stake here', announced Secretary for State for Northern Ireland, Humphrey Atkins. Just before Christmas 1980 the British government presented a document to the prisoners which appeared to form the basis of a settlement. It depended on which way the document was interpreted. The prisoners in the Blocks ended their fast, presuming that they had won their battle. But the prison authorities chose to interpret the document narrowly, especially in relation to the men wearing their own clothes. This was the most sensitive issue. If prisoners wore their own clothes, they could then wash them whenever they wished. That would give them a measure of freedom and dignity which a convict's uniform would not.

The hunger strikers went to the brink, gained concessions and then found out that the 'agreement' wasn't worth the paper it was written on. It must have seemed that the prisoners would not have the heart or the will for a second hunger strike. Logistically, a second hunger strike would be much more difficult. It would be harder to get public support and people might have to die to prove the point this time. The second hunger strike started on 1 March 1981. Bobby Sands was the first man on. The men demanded the right to wear their own clothes, the right to free association, the right to normal visits, letters and parcels, the right to refuse to do prison work and the restoration of remission lost through protests. This second strike was different. Men would join the strike at strategic intervals. The men in the Blocks pushed the hunger strike. The leadership of the republican movement on the outside was against it since the strike had the potential for hijacking the entire movement. As the strike moved forward the battle lines were being drawn. The issues, which might seem relatively trivial to outsiders, were of fundamental importance to men confined to prison, where the world becomes a much smaller place. Humphrey Atkins told the House of Commons in London that 'The principles by which the Government has stood in the face of the protests at the Maze and Armagh prisons still stand. It will not concede that it should now establish within the normal Northern Ireland prison regime a special set of conditions for particular groups of prisoners.' He added that 'The Government will not surrender control of what goes on in the prisons to a particular group of prisoners. It will not concede the demand for political status, or recognise that murder and violence are less culpable because they are claimed to be committed for political motives.' In Armagh jail women had been on the same political status protest as the men in the Blocks (though the issue here was not the prison uniform since women prisoners could wear their own clothes, but it was made worse by menstrual blood being smeared on the walls).

As the marches and protests started to get under way on the outside, four H-Block activists were shot dead by Protestant paramilitaries—the UVF and UFF. The first man on the strike, Bobby Sands, was elected to the House of Commons for the constituency of Fermanagh/South Tyrone, polling 30,492 votes. Against the better judgment of some of the republican leadership, he ran and won. Sands continued to die day by day, little by little. The prison authorities and warders in the Blocks were shattered. The hunger strikes were broadening the battlefield for the Provos, and they were becoming something more than cheerleaders for the IRA. Bobby Sands was the first to die, and he was followed by nine more, in all, seven IRA men and three INLA men. The sound of the trolleys bearing the dead men coming from the prison hospital was an enduring sound that many prisoners were to remember.

National and international support for the hunger strikers was unprecedented, and the British authorities came under increasing pressure. The British government, while stating publicly that it would not concede the demands, was secretly negotiating with representatives of the IRA on the outside.

14

Rioting followed each of the deaths. Fifty-one people were killed, including ten police and thirteen soldiers. More than 1,000 people were injured, 1,700 were arrested and thousands of plastic bullets were fired on the streets. Despite the public posturing, the British had once again talked to the IRA. Clergymen and relatives intervened in the strike and it came to an end. With the exception of the no-work issue, the demands were effectively conceded.

Relations within the Blocks were very bad. When Bobby Sands died warders were said to have taunted the prisoners and made jokes about the dead man. There were similar incidents following the other nine deaths. The five years of bitter protest had brought together, and merged, two differing views within the Provos—traditional militant nationalists and more radically inclined socialists. The combination was to change the face of the Provos, especially in the way they would choose to move forward after the strike. The traditional diehard attitude was tempered by the realisation that there was a need for compromise, especially with those who had taken no part in the protest and needed to be wooed back to the movement. Throughout the hunger strike the prisoners had been represented by Brendan McFarlane, who was a key figure. The British had considered him the 'soft underbelly' of the strike. His friends were dying, they expected him to compromise on principles. His soft manner belied a very tough outlook indeed.

One of three children, Brendan McFarlane was born in Ardoyne in 1951. He was nicknamed Bik in school, after a brand of biscuit. His father worked in Michelin's tyre factory in Belfast. His family especially his mother, was very religious. He stood out at school both mentally and physically, and through a family friendship with a Catholic priest called Fr Marcelles Bik decided to become a priest. He joined up with the SVD missionaries in Wales and began to study in their seminary. He believed that he had a vocation. His friends were very surprised at his decision as he was not openly very religious. And, in fact, when he came on holidays from time to time, he didn't conform to the image of the stuffy priest; on the contrary, he liked going out. He was home on holiday in 1969 when Ardoyne was attacked by loyalist mobs. He returned to Wales, spending two years in all there, but he left the seminary in 1970, and never could give a clear answer as to why he did. He did not immediately become involved with the IRA. He had friends in both the Official and Provisional IRA at the time and didn't know which to join, but following internment in 1971 he joined the Provos. Three days after internment was introduced, in August 1971, he was arrested during a gun battle in which two British soldiers were killed. But generally he never came under suspicion. He was involved in defending the area at a time when IRA slogans were daubed over to read 'I Ran Away'. The Green Howard Regiment patrolled Ardoyne, but were unable to subdue the area. He worked in a printing firm in Belfast, and then in 1973 got a job driving a fork lift. He was very active in the IRA.

Many of his friends were killed. In 1972 a gun battle started between the Provos and loyalists. The loyalists attacked people coming out of the drinking clubs and part of McFarlane's job was to make sure they got out safely. When the Provos returned fire the British Army suddenly joined in and opened up from three machine-gun positions. Two men died that night and the gun battle raged for hours. Both were close friends of McFarlane's. It was 1974 before McFarlane came under suspicion again, and he was arrested a few times that year. The following year a truce was called between the British Army and the IRA with the latter setting up their own 'incident centres' with direct links to the security forces in the event of a breach. Loyalist assassination squads started to work on what they saw as a sell-out and sectarian assassinations followed. In July 1975 four soldiers were killed in South Armagh in reprisal for two Provos killed in Divis Flats in Belfast. The first day of August saw the Miami Showband gunned down as they returned from playing at a dance in Banbridge, County Down. More and more no-warning bomb attacks were taking place in Loyalist and nationalist areas across the North. On 13 August, the Bayardo bar was attacked.

The Bayardo was a bar in a loyalist area of Belfast used by the UVF as a rendezvous. Four men drove up in a car. Gunfire raked the front of the bar as the man in the passenger seat ran into the hallway and planted a smoking duffle bag containing a bomb. There were about sixty people there. Three died in the explosion and two were killed by gunfire. The car used in the attacked was stopped minutes afterwards and Bik McFarlane was seen to be driving. Peter Hamilton and Seamus Clarke were also picked up. All three were charged and convicted, and were recommended to serve no less than twenty-five years in prison. They were due for release in the year 2001. After four years on active service McFarlane was locked away. He was put into Cage 11 Long Kesh and life was fairly relaxed. Contact with warders was fairly minimal. McFarlane was highly politicised, articulate and educated. He identified more with the revolutionary South American priest Camillo Torres who had set aside the cassock in favour of the gun. He failed to get out of the Cages with Papillon and Pat McGeown, lost his political status and ended up in the Blocks.

McFarlane was the type of person who had the ability to instil a lot of confidence in people around him. He played music well and appeared to know exactly what he was doing even when he didn't. Everything he did, he did efficiently, and without fuss. During the hunger strikes, he wrote thousands of communications—better known as comms—to the men on the inside and to the leadership on the outside. He managed to write them at night by the orange light that came into his cell through the cracks in the door. The comms were written on cigarette papers, and wrapped in cling film wrappers. They could fit anywhere, up your nose, between your teeth, under your foreskin, up your back passage. They were passed from cell to cell by a small space left between the heating pipes for expansion. Women carried them in and out of the jail on visits.

Lifers on the inside would put up a fight if a warder tried to take a comm off them—if it was important enough. They had nothing to lose by getting another twenty years. The warders know about the comms, but didn't bother that much about them.

McFarlane was always approachable and very good at diplomacy. While he was capable of manipulating people towards the end of a goal, he personally would find enormous difficulty in being false. It would bother him. When the hunger strike was over, he was drained physically and emotionally and he decided to step down from the leadership of the Provos within Long Kesh. The Provos faced major problems within the prison: morale was at an all-time low and the republican prisoners were divided as many had not taken part in the protests. There was a considerable amount of bitterness towards the men who had opted out. And there was also a lot of guilt among some of the men. They had seen their friends die,

17

and now they were still alive. Their feelings were mixed—relief at being alive, but guilt at having lived through it all.

The hunger strike ended on 5 October 1981. The IRA had placed active service units in Britain during the previous year, and five days later they struck. On that Saturday they parked a laundry van close to Chelsea barracks in London, the head-quarters of the First Battalion, Irish Guards Regiment. At 11.30 am, two IRA members pushed the van into position 100 yards from the barracks' gate. Forty minutes later a bus carrying soldiers from ceremonial duties at the Tower of London slowed down to squeeze past the van and the IRA used a command wire to detonate the bomb inside. There was nothing left of the van but the frame as the bus careered across the road. Two civilians were killed and twenty-two soldiers wounded. One week later, Lieutenant-General Sir Stuart Pringle of the Royal Marine Commandos, who had served twice in the North, drove his red Volkswagen from his home at South Croxten Road, a few miles from Chelsea barracks. The bomb in his car went off almost immediately.

Nine days later Reuters News Agency in London got a phone call at 2.50 pm. There were three bombs near Oxford Street—at the Wimpy Bar, Debenham's and Bourne's. Thousands were immediately cleared from the area. Minutes later a landrover drove up to the Wimpy Bar and a stout middle-aged man jumped from it. He laughed and joked with the police about bomb scares as he put on his padded vest and helmet. He picked up his bag but couldn't get in the door of the bar as it was locked. It was opened for him but none of the scores of people milling about outside took much notice of him. Then all the windows of the bar suddenly came onto the street. The Wimpy Bar sign fell off the front of the shop and there was smoke everywhere. One policeman put his head in his hands and just shook it. He couldn't believe it. The bomb disposal expert had found the five-pound bomb at precisely 3.43 pm and was killed instantly. There was a twelve-foot hole in the pavement. The glass shattered across Oxford Street. The tube running underneath had to be diverted. Buses were rerouted and cars were abandoned in panic. Rush-hour traffic was reduced to chaos. The Debenham's bomb was defused and Bourne's was sealed off.

Two weeks later a bomb at the home of the British Attorney General Sir Michael Havers exploded half an hour before midnight. There was nobody in the house at the time. His Wimbledon home had been under round-the-clock surveillance by the police. A policewoman outside the flat was treated for shock.

The attacks in Britain were a measure of the anger felt at the way the Prime Minister Margaret Thatcher had handled the hunger strike. The IRA made it clear that they regarded her as personally responsible for the deaths of ten men. But there was still the row within the prisons to be resolved. The two wars were equally bitter.

Three men from H5 were on the Boards for speaking Irish to warders. They had refused as a matter of principle to speak to them in English. The Boards was the name given to the punishment cells, concrete boxes with concrete beds a few inches off the ground. There is a heater high up on the walls, which has what looks like a steel sheet in front of it. There was a constant drone from the heater, the sound of it drummed inside your skull twenty-four hours a day. And there was the window with bars and thick glass you couldn't see through and no communication with other prisoners. The Boards were fairly full after the hunger strike. One man was there for months; he refused to do prison work, and then he would get three days on the Boards. When the three days were over, he would be offered work. He'd refuse again, three more days on the Boards. This went on and on for months; they were trying to break him. The warders in each Block had also decided that it would be a good idea to get the prisoners to paint each of their Wings. They were looking for four volunteers from each Wing to carry out the work. The warders were determined to get the prisoners to work. The men weren't too happy about forced prison work, which would seek to criminalise them. Serious trouble was brewing in the Blocks. New thinking was called for, if the Provos were ever to get anywhere. At the end of 1981, they had two choices. They could continue to refuse stubbornly to cooperate, or they could continue the no-work protest and stay in their cells and lose remission. They had gained most of what they wanted. They would have to find a way out of the impasse. But if anything was to be done it would have to be done quickly.

2

The Blanket Men are Coming

It was 6 January 1982. The two republican orderlies moved slowly through the wings of H6. Orderlies were in a privileged position—they had access throughout a Block where they worked. Only prisoners who conformed could be orderlies. It was late afternoon when the two men dispensed the tea and cake to the men. A warder followed them; he didn't like what he saw. They were giving out large pieces of cake to prisoners. He thought they were too big and he demanded that they cut the cake in two and divide it. The two orderlies ignored him; the warder ordered them to cut the cake again. They ignored him. They thought it was a bit of a laugh really. Then they ended up on the Boards for refusing to obey the order.

The new year had not taken any bitterness out of the situation, either inside or outside the jail. Two days later, it was just after 9 a.m. when a hijacked car drove onto the forecourt of the Castleton Filling Station on the Antrim Road in Belfast. An IRA man got out and shot the station attendant six times. He was a part-time member of the UDR and had started work at the station only that week. As the snow started to fall the six-person IRA unit made their getaway in another hijacked car.

Five hours later, when the statement admitting IRA responsibility had been telexed from the Press Centre on the Falls Road, the building was surrounded by British Army and RUC. All roads to the area were sealed off and it took the RUC twenty-five minutes to sledge in the door of the building. Seven people were held for forty-eight hours for questioning.

But if Sinn Féin were coming under increasing pressure from the British Army, the British authorities were also still taking heavy flak from the hunger strike. The Russian newspaper *Pravda* said that the British cried 'crocodile tears' for human

20

rights throughout the world while they submitted their political opponents to 'unbearable humiliation' by throwing them into prison. The British, the paper went on, operated a 'system of moral terror'. And despite the fact that the Russians themselves were less than snow-white when it came to human rights, the rebuke must have been embarrassing for the British.

Then two loyalists in the Blocks went on hunger strike. They wanted segregation from republican prisoners. This was the start of a battle which was to be bitter and to last eighteen months. If republican prisoners came off protest, they would be required to do prison work, effectively to conform. It would be a hard decision with the memory of the ten men dead still fresh in their minds. Conforming would also mean going into mixed Blocks with loyalists. The thinking behind mixed Blocks was that neither side could control them, and therefore the authorities controlled them. The first loyalist onto the hunger strike was UDA man James Watson, in for the attempted murder of Bernadette McAliskey who as Bernadette Devlin (her maiden name) became MP for Mid-Ulster at twenty-one. The second was UVF man Adrian Dowds, in on a similiar charge. UDA leader John McMichael announced that there would be others going on hunger strike. It was ironic that the loyalists were now following the same type of protest the republicans had engaged in during previous years, and for which republicans had been accused of trying to bring civil war to the North. But the line of thought within the republican camp was changing.

Discussion and debate started about coming off the no-work protest. By refusing to work, men were locked in their cells, and were going nowhere. The loyalists weren't too happy to hear that the Provos were coming off their protest. They had a vision of these men, who had lived in their own filth for five years, smeared their body secretions on their cell walls, refused to wash, and finally starved themselves to death when all else failed. The loyalists took the view that these men were totally crazy and having them in the same Block was bad news. The word went out to the loyalists; the blanket men are coming. The Provos were using the reputation of the protesters to frighten the loyalists.

The Provos adopted a new strategy. But before that happened, Brendan McFarlane, emotionally drained, had stepped down as OC of the camp and was replaced by Sid Walsh, who was extremely capable. He had been jailed in January 1973 and served three years. In August 1976 he was jailed again. He was intelligent and articulate and respected within the movement. His task was to work on the concessions gained during the hunger strike—clothes, parcels and visits, limited association. The arguments for and against coming off were bitter and divisive. Those who wanted to continue thought it was a sell-out to the men who had died to end the protest. The opposite camp argued that nothing could move forward until the men left their cells, and if that meant working, then so be it. The idea was to build on what they had gained. Six men were handpicked to leave the protest. They became known, as did those immediately following them, as the South Atlantic Task Force, after the British Fleet which took four weeks to sail around the world to retake the Falklands from Argentina. The idea was also starting to ferment that segregation could be gained by getting the loyalists to go on protests; by getting the loyalists to go on protests, the loyalists would be moved to other Blocks and that would be effective segregation, if by another name. To do that, the Provos would have to threaten and intimidate them. But as yet, they weren't in a position to do that.

The plan was that men would be ordered off the protest in a disciplined way, with a specific aim in view and a specific tactical blueprint for achieving their aims. The fact was that the Provos were also split; they were split into those who had protested and those who had not taken part in any protest. It was decided by the leadership, on the outside and inside, that the men coming off protest should now go in with the conforming prisoners, rather than the other way around. A community spirit would have to be built from scratch.

Pat McGeown, the man who had tried to escape with McFarlane and Papillon was a key figure within the jail. He was a small man who had been interned first when he was sixteen years old. Liked and very much respected within the Provos, he had been jailed for blowing up the Europa Hotel in Belfast in January 1975. At the time it was the most bombed hotel in the North. Following the unsuccessful escape attempt, he had ended up in the Blocks, on the blanket, on hunger strike. Medical problems prevented him from going on with his fast. He was a firm believer in always keeping all options open until such time as they had to be closed off. He now argued to get out of the cells.

22

It took eight months to feel any tangible result of the new strategy. It was a slow process, building piece by piece. The battle over segregation was brutal and dramatic. And in the end the Provos and loyalists would push events so fast that the prison authorities would not be able to keep track of what was happening.

On one Block, UVF man Lennie Murphy was the OC. He was particularly feared because of his association with the Shankill Butchers, a notorious loyalist gang that had tortured and killed Catholics in random sectarian attacks. Three members of the Butcher gang were on the same Wing as Murphy. The Provos sent out part of their Task Force, and the new Provo OC arrived on the Wing. Of the thirty-nine men in the Wing, only thirteen were republican, and of those thirteen, six were happy to serve their sentences in peace and wanted no part in confrontation.

Seamus Campbell was the OC. Campbell was from County Tyrone and had joined the Fianna, the junior wing of the IRA, in 1972. It took him five years to graduate to the IRA and he was fairly active. He operated out of Omagh and didn't come under suspicion for years. It was after 1977 that he began to get arrested on a frequent basis and spent a lot of time in Gough Barracks. He claimed he was beaten in custody, and Amnesty International looked at his case at one point. It was around that time that the allegations of routine beatings taking place in Gough Barracks began to emerge. Later these allegations were to be substantiated. On one of his arrests in 1977, Campbell said he was burned with cigarettes. He continued his IRA activities and by June 1980 he was a qualified mechanic working in his father's garage in Coalisland. He got a call from a wellknown customer about a lorry that was broken down a short distance from Coalisland. He went to the lorry, and then left the area to get tools to do work on it. When he returned the lorry was surrounded by RUC and British Army. Guns were trained on him. Campbell was sure that he was going to be shot dead, the police had told him often enough that they would shoot him. A local farmer came around the corner and the Army lowered their weapons. They asked Campbell what he was doing. He said he'd come to fix the lorry. They asked who owned the lorry; he told them; they said they didn't believe him. There was a bomb buried under a load of clay on the lorry, and Campbell was arrested, together with several people in the area. He was subsequently charged with possession of the explosives and was remanded to Crumlin Road Jail. He applied twice in the following eighteen months for bail but was refused. Thirteen policemen gave evidence at his trial. The prosecution produced 144 pages of alleged verbal statements made by Campbell while in custody. A verbal statement is a statement made by a suspect in custody. An alleged verbal statement is a statement said by the police to have been made by a suspect to the police while in custody but later denied by the suspect. Campbell said he had said nothing in custody. The judge decided to believe the verbals as told by the police. The trial lasted three weeks. There were discrepancies; one such was when the RUC said they had the lorry under surveillance and that they knew whom it belonged to. They said they knew because of the nameplate on the front of the lorry. There was no such nameplate on the lorry, but it didn't make any difference in the end and Campbell was sent down for possession and membership. A conspiracy charge was dropped. He continued to protest, saying he knew nothing about the explosives. He got fourteen years. He continued to protest his innocence in jail, but to no avail. And now he was in the same Wing as Lennie Murphy, talking to him. Murphy wanted to know what was going on. What was happening with the blanket men? Why were they coming onto the Block? Campbell, in his quiet Tyrone accent, informed him that the blanket men were, in a word, mad. They were all coming off the protest, and they were making plans. He remained obscure about these plans.

There were two republican lifers at the end of one Wing and they had more or less opted out of the Provos. They were content to serve their sentence. The Provos floated the rumour that loyalists were about to start killing republicans on the Block. Campbell went to Murphy again, and demanded clarification of the position. Murphy said it was a lie, there was no plan to kill Provos. The two lifers at the end of the Wing were pointed out as Provo 'sleepers' and Murphy was told that if anything happened to any Provo on the Block, the two had nothing to lose, were quite ruthless and had orders to kill Murphy himself. The two lifers had no idea they were being used in this game.

There was a genuine fear among the Provos that the loyalists would start to attack them. A loyalist could stab any one of them with a steel comb while he was walking past and nobody would ever know who did it.

On one Wing of a Block there were just four Provos and they lived in fear of their lives. All four were forced to live as a unit, not letting each other out of sight at any time. There was a good chance that one would be beaten or killed if they did. The Provos used their best men on their Task Force.

Padraig McKearney was born and reared in County Tyrone and went to primary schools in College Land and The Moy. He went on to Dungannon Academy, but dropped out when he was first arrested in 1972, at the age of seventeen. He was charged with blowing up Moy Post Office in County Tyrone. He was badly beaten by soldiers and spent six weeks on remand at Crumlin Road Jail before the charges were dropped through lack of evidence. At the end of 1973 he was sentenced to seven years for the possession of the weapons. He came from a very strong republican family. His brother was killed on active service with the IRA in May and his elder brother was also in the Blocks with him. His sister was forced to live in the South on the run. Padraig McKearney was caught again in 1980 and got fourteen years. He had a developed political perspective, and was considered an out-and-out communist. He read quite a bit and was respected among the men in the Blocks. The impact he made when he came off the protest was quite significant. As McKearney came off the protest, one warder remarked to him 'This must be the final push for Port Stanley.'

Meanwhile, the Provos were still talking. Murphy was getting worried and wondered how to get segregation. The Provos presented a plan to him. In one discussion, he was advised to place a bomb under his own bed, and blame it on the Provos. It could then be claimed that the Provos were trying to kill them and would get moved to another Wing. They would be segregated. The Provos even offered to make up the bomb. It was a simple affair—lighter fuel petrol, a bulb and a bucket. The bomb was made up and delivered to the loyalists. But it didn't end up under Murphy's bed. It was decided that the best place to place it was under the bed of a UVF man who had been jailed with offences linked to the Kincora Boys Home scandal. He had also been involved with Tara, a shadowy loyalist paramilitary organisation. The man was treated with a sort of reverence by the warders and to the Provos at least he seemed to have some sort of hold over the warders. He was an ideal victim for the bomb, because if he were brought into line, the warders would follow.

The bomb was taken by the UVF man to his cell just before lock-up one afternoon. There were two men in the cell. But just before the doors were locked, something seemed to click. It began to dawn on the two men in the cell that if the bomb went off while they were locked in, they might get burned. Suddenly, one of them jumped up from his bed and ran down the corridor shouting 'bomb, bomb, bomb'. The entire Wing was evacuated, and the two UVF men were taken to the Boards as punishment. They were accused of planting the bomb themselves and were charged with possession. Papillon laughed.

Men were sent into segregated Wings with the loyalists; immediately they started to engineer themselves into a position where the loyalists would fear them. Day by day they pushed farther and farther to the point where the loyalists were terrified and were in real fear of their lives. It was mainly through the use of incidents such as the bombs in the cells, and the threats of incidents, that control would have to be gained. As the tension grew, the Provos thought they had a psychological advantage over both the prison authorities and the loyalists. Neither group wanted a confrontation. The Provos kept pointing to some of their own 'hard men' and what they were capable of. The Provos wanted segregation, and they were going to get it.

Shortly after the bombing incident, loyalists in some Wings were advised by the Provos to smash their cells. Smashing their cells meant that they would be moved. The loyalist OC went to the Provos in one Wing and said they were going to wreck the entire Block on one particular night. The Provos asked if they were going to wreck all cells. The loyalists said that if all their men didn't co-operate, they would deal with them themselves. All cells with the exception of two were wrecked. The two remaining loyalists didn't want to get a hard time from the warders for destroying their cells. They both had a short time left to serve and didn't want to lose their remission by misbehaving. The Provos told one of them that they were going to be killed.

That night the Provos shouted from Wing to Wing, communicating in Irish. The order went out in Irish that the two men were to be beaten up. The Provo OC of the Wing broke into English, pretending not to understand the orders in Irish. He

26

roared back up the Block. Were the two loyalists to be killed? Papillon could be heard laughing away to himself. The orders came back. No, the two were not to be killed. The order to kill all remaining loyalists was rescinded, the loyalists should be beaten up instead. There was a stillness and a silence in the Block. Suddenly, the sound of a cell being smashed up could be heard. The entire Block erupted in laughter. The Provos had control, the two loyalists were gone. But if segregation was achieved in many cases with only the threat of violence, it was actual violence in other cases which secured the Blocks.

On one occasion the loyalists beat up an IRSP man and the Provos went to the loyalists and told them they were no longer going to recognise their structures on account of this unacceptable behaviour. The meeting took place between the Provos and the loyalists with the Provos being backed up by a man fresh off the blanket, with a baton shoved down the back of his trousers. The loyalists wanted to know why he was carrying a baton. 'Just in case' the answer came back. The blanket man stood and glared and said nothing. And then the Provos moved in on the UVF commander an hour later and beat him up. Throughout H-Blocks 6, 7 and 8, the loyalists started to refuse to leave their cells. They started to lose remission of their sentence. Only Provo orderlies were moving freely through the Blocks, and the Provos started up the rumour machine again to the effect that the food was poisoned, washing powder was thrown across it and the republicans refused to eat it. The loyalists were terrified and stopped eating. Some loyalists who had only a short time left to serve and didn't want to lose their remission took themselves off to the hospital for the duration of the protest. Other loyalists were told that unless they co-operated with the Provos in their plans for segregation they would be killed as soon as they were released. The battle was long and hard and still the Provos were a long way off winning. But they were getting there.

Then the loyalists started to slop out through the grilles on the doors of their cells. More threats were issued—if they didn't leave the Blocks they would be killed after forty-eight hours. Unionist politician Peter Robinson visited the loyalist prisoners. The Governor said that segregation was not going to be conceded. But as soon as the slop-out protest started, the loyalists had to be moved as they constituted a health hazard.

The Provos had used their remand prisoners to persuade the

protesting republicans to come off protests. 1981 had been a bad year for the Provos. Dozens of IRA men were picked up on operations in Belfast, and paid informers were naming names. By 1982, many of those remand prisoners were convicted and were starting to serve their sentences. They were encouraged to join the protesting men, with a view to persuading those still protesting to end it. Their intervention was crucial in persuading many to come out of their cells. They argued that the men should leave their cells, use the prison system and prepare themselves for their eventual release. The four weeks that new prisoners spent on committal wings were spent arguing with the protesters. The strategy worked. Towards the end developments within the prison moved very fast, the prison authorities were unable to keep up with them. The final push was quite a bit up the road but in the end would only take a week.

The traditional Provo structures within prisons were clear cut. They were hierarchical and rigid. The main thrust placed great emphasis on accepting orders from above. Now that started to change. More emphasis was placed on the republican community. Ordinary criminals within the Blocks, with no connections with the republican movement, were encouraged to become involved in debates and lectures and sports activities. And when the Provos finally went to work there were other problems.

Different work was rewarded with different rates of pay. The Provos decided that this was potentially divisive and they pooled all monies earned in this way. Everybody was paid the same from this common pool of money, no matter where they were working. Co-ops were set up, and while this might appear a small thing in itself, it was important to encourage a spirit of co-operation. On 4 November 1982 the no-work protest was officially ended and this allowed selected and committed Provos onto the Blocks with a specific purpose. Many prisoners were still resisting coming off the six-year protest. On that date the Provos were offered work throughout the prison. But it didn't quite work out as the prison authorities had planned. There was the concrete yard. This was considered the prison equivalent of outer Siberia by the prison authorities but the men liked it there. It was a wide open space close to the M1 motorway and plans for escape could be hatched without much hindrance from the authorities and there was less supervision. On arrival at the

concrete yard the Provos were obliged to make various worthwhile items, such as garden gnomes. They were showed how to
mix sand and cement and water, and in what proportions. But
somehow, it never seemed to work out. There was too much
water, or too much sand, and the gnomes just fell to pieces. It
wasn't that the Provos were refusing to work, but well, it just
didn't seem to work out. Productivity was very low. In the metal
fabrication shops prisoners were shown again and again how to
make the frames for the chairs and tables they were supposed to
be manufacturing. But they never seemed to get the hang of it.
The pieces would be too long, or too short, or wouldn't fit. In the
stitching workshop they were shown again and again how to use
the machines. Thud! As soon as the warder's back was turned
the sound of a snarled-up machine could be heard. 'Are you
stupid?' the prisoner would be asked. 'Yes,' came the reply.
Everybody was working but nothing was happening. Bits went
missing from machines. The necessary quota of chairs or tables
or garden gnomes was sometimes made by the warders themselves. Anything for a quiet life.

The sabotage continued on a massive scale until such time as
attempts to get the Provos to conform ceased. The Provos got
their way without open confrontation. But the real bonuses
related to the fact that there were men from different Blocks
coming together for the first time in years. The prisoners were
also seeing the prison for the first time. They could see the
security gates and the watch towers and they began to think of
ways to get out. For the first time in years their heads were being
turned towards escaping. They knew very little about the camp
at this point and even the layout was a mystery. But they began
to gather information, and ideas came together.

There were a lot of lifers going to the workshops. Some of
them got the idea that they could make escape implements.
They started to make replica weapons, hooks, keys, jemmies,
knives, all quite openly. The order came down to stop all of that.
If the workshops were stopped because of some hairbrained
scheme, nothing would be gained. The dog-eat-dog mentality
within the Blocks was still prevalent, although changes could be
seen. A failed escape attempt, no matter how small, would be
very bad for morale. It would also have the effect of making the
authorities look at all the security loopholes and close them off.
Combined with this, morale within the IRA on the outside was

bad, and a botched escape would make it worse. But some lifers, who were stopped from making their tools in the workshop were quite resentful of the orders. They were lifers with no chance of release and they took the view that they had the right to be the first ones to try and escape.

On the outside, support was still high for the Provos. In October 1982 they held ten per cent of the vote in the Assembly Elections, and took five seats; Gerry Adams, Danny Morrison, Jim McAllister, Owen Carron and Martin McGuinness were all elected. However, on a military level things were sliding downhill with one disaster after another.

First of all, there were the informers. They sowed seeds of suspicion and doubt among activists. The fact that one day people were carrying out operations as a unit and the following day one member of that unit was naming all the others in court had a bad effect on morale. It was hard to trust people. Then there was the shoot-to-kill policy which cropped up again in November 1982. Between 1969 and 1982 at least 150 unarmed people had been shot dead by the British Army, RUC and UDR, in disputed circumstances. But towards the end of that year it appeared that shooting people dead was being pursued as a deliberate policy.

It was just before 7pm on 11 November 1982 when Sean Burns and Eugene Toman returned to Lurgan in County Armagh. Both were Provos, and Burns had been identified on an operation and was on the run. On this Thursday evening, both men sneaked back into the town and drove to Gervais McKerr's house. McKerr was also in the IRA. Burns and Toman had something to eat and laughed and joked with a young woman who was in the house. As they waited for a safe car to take them to a safe house for the night, McKerr decided that he would drive the two himself in his Ford Escort. A short distance from the house, at Tullygally Road East, three RUC men ambushed the car and fired 108 bullets into it. The three men were killed instantly. The full truth of the killing was never revealed by the RUC. They said there was a roadblock and that the Escort had driven through it, they said they had only opened fire when they believed their lives were in danger. The press releases were all misleading. McKerr's house was raided immediately after the killing but his wife was not told that Gervais was dead. A priest told her six hours later. All three were unarmed.

The next killing took place thirteen days later and related to a previous Provo operation. MI5 had bugged a hayshed belonging to the widow of a republican who lived just outside Lurgan. The Provos managed to sneak explosives into the shed while there was surveillance on it, and they sneaked the explosives out again, without being noticed. Even though the entire area was on high alert, three RUC men were given clearance to go in. They were told that the explosives were still in the shed. All three RUC men were killed in a landmine explosion which followed. The RUC mounted further surveillance on the shed. There were three 60-year-old rifles in there. Michael Tighe and Martin McCauley arrived at the shed, having been asked to keep an eye on it by the widow. They noticed a window open and climbed in. The RUC opened fire. Tighe was killed and McCauley was wounded. Both were unarmed. Michael Tighe had no connections with any paramilitary organisation. A tape recording of the entire incident was held by the RUC and they afterwards refused to hand it over to the British policeman, John Stalker who was investigating the shoot-to-kill policy.

Then in early December Seamus Grew and Roddy Carroll, two INLA men, were driving to their homes at Mullacreevia Park in Armagh City. A car sped past them as they went up the hill, pulled up in front and an RUC constable got out and shot both unarmed men dead. The entire area had been cordoned off. The two men had been followed for days, without any attempt being made to arrest them. An RUC man was finally charged with the murder of Seamus Grew and was acquitted. Mr Justice MacDermott held that the RUC man had used reasonable force in the circumstances. The RUC said the car had gone through a roadblock and that they had opened fire to protect the lives of RUC men. Again, the press releases were misleading. The net effect of the killings was to suggest that Provo and INLA men were going to be shot on sight. But if things were going bad on the outside, they were picking up inside the Blocks.

Bik McFarlane was appointed orderly in late 1982. This allowed him to move freely around his Block. If the Provos were to get anywhere they would have to get the structures to suit themselves. In this they were assisted to a certain degree by the warders themselves. For five years the Provos had waged their battles. The warders just wanted to do their job and draw their pay. When they saw the Provos starting to conform they were very reluctant to rock the boat on what were, after all, relatively minor issues. They began to recognise the Provo structures within the prison. If a warder went to a Provo he would be referred to the OC of the Wing or the Block and the warder would go off and find the OC. Even those in senior positions within the prison began to accept the practice. While making a tour of the Blocks, senior prison staff would just 'happen' to drop in on the OC to see how things were going. But it was not always that easy. Sometimes there were stand-off situations between the prisoners and the riot squads. The prisoners would refuse to lock up on a jail issue and would push it as far as necessary. One of those issues related to a certain number of warders who were totally unacceptable to the prisoners. They had behaved badly during the hunger strikes and were thought to be of a confrontational frame of mind. The Provos told the prison authorities that these men were unacceptable on the Wings and that their safety could not be guaranteed. Generally they were kept well away from the men; they were placed in positions where their contact with prisoners was minimal and there could be no flashpoint. But sometimes, if there was an awkward senior officer on, he might decide to place these men in sensitive positions, behaviour which the Provos took to be deliberately provocative. Then the men would refuse to lock up. And then the riot squad would arrive at the entrance to the Block and a stand-off would develop. It never came to the squad being sent in but there were some near confrontations. On one occasion, the warders called for a head count in one Block. The prisoners refused to move, and said they could be counted were they stood. The prison authorities backed off. But gradually the cumulative effect of all of this was to give the men more and more freedom and say in the running of the Blocks. And through those developments the Provos could also nominate who would fill key orderly positions in the Blocks. They would send a name to the authorities, and the authorities might come back and say that the person nominated was unacceptable. The Provos would reply that nobody else was prepared to take the job. Inevitably the authorities relented. Lifers were considered unacceptable for orderly positions. But because there was no work in the workshops and they were filled to overflowing with conforming prisoners who did virtually nothing, more and more orderly positions were created to keep the men busy. In some instances, the lengths to which the men tried to 'educate' themselves was farcical. The men took correspondence courses, and some of them made an application to do an electronics course. It was fairly simply stuff—fixing washing machines and cars. But the application was turned down. There was a limit. That limit appeared to be stopping short of teaching the men skills which they could employ usefully should they return to active service.

But it was to be 1983 before the no-work protest was aired in public by the Provos. Jim Gibney wrote to the official paper of the republican movement, *An Phoblacht/Republican News*, and outlined the position within Long Kesh. There were still 250 men on protest. He asked a question. He wanted to know if the time had come for all no-work protest to end, so that men and women serving sentences could see an end to their sentence with the restoration of remission. They were doubling their sentences every day they spent on protest. He said the main issue was segregation and work. But he argued that the prison authorities had already conceded segregation for remand prisoners and that it would take very little to spread this throughout the prison. This was the public explanation of what was happening in the Blocks. In order to assure people on the outside, and supporters, that the men on the inside were not going soft and conforming, they had to present an explicable policy. There had to be rational reasons for what was to follow. It was in this context that the Escape Committee was born, with Papillon in charge.

Traditionally, all escape ideas went through the normal command structures, on up the line. But some of those command structures had been in place a long time, and some of the men had been in prison too long. New ideas were needed. New people were brought onto the Committee. The new structure was more lateral and gave easier access. Ideas were passed through the Wing OCs and Block OCs. The Committee itself comprised no more than five people. It liaised directly with the outside. All escape ideas had to go through the Committee. This was to be particularly significant later on. And it was towards the end of that year that Papillon came across a friendly face in the kitchen. 'If I was still trying to escape', he told a friend, 'this would be a gift.' He had only a couple of years to do.

It wouldn't be worth his while trying to get away now. If he was caught, the price would be too high.

Several people were telling Papillon things. Men were coming up to him and explaining about this food lorry that went around the camp three times a day, every day, all year. One man came up with the idea of taking the food lorry as far as the kitchen, and then getting into a rubbish lorry and getting dumped out in the country. Another Provo remarked to Papillon that it would be possible to take the gym bus and drive from the prison. Papillon told them all that their ideas were nuts, hairbrained, to forget them. Life just wasn't like that. There was nothing in it, said Papillon, it just wasn't possible to drive out of the prison.

Bobby Storey was fairly fresh, he hadn't been in the Blocks very long. He had come in in 1981 and the Provos on the outside knew what his capabilities were. Any escape would have to be backed by the people on the outside. Their back-up in terms of personnel and weapons and safe houses would be crucial. And if the men on the inside were talking escapes seriously, they would have to have a person whom the outside knew and trusted to talk on their behalf. Storey was just such a man. He ended up in the same Block as Bik McFarlane. And more ideas started to get thrown around. Storey wasn't too meticulous, but he was known as a man who got things done, a pusher. The idea started to float around that it was possible to take a Block, to take it over. Papillon was given the idea. He put the idea of the lorry and the taking of the Block together. He had the basis of a big escape but still nothing very solid. He started to work on the basis that it was possible to take the entire prison—all eight Blocks. He worked on the basis that it was possible, in theory at least, to get everybody out of the prison.

Within the Blocks themselves, there were other strange developments over a period of months in 1982. Suddenly, the prisoners started to co-operate with warders, they started to build up personal relationships with them. This was easier than it might first appear. When the blanket men said they were conforming, many warders thought that the prisoners would try and take revenge for the way some of them had been treated during the hunger strikes. The warders were very apprehensive as they watched the men come off in twos and threes. The warders had a grudging respect for the Provos—they had stuck to their principles—and they knew what they were capable of. They thought there would be revenge on a massive scale. Indeed, many Provos wanted revenge. A decision was taken. By playing a different sort of game, the prisoners might get further; by doing what the warders didn't expect, perhaps it could lead to other things.

When the warders were greeted by friendly faces, many jumped at the chance of squaring up everything and settling past differences. It was with a sense of relief that many warders discovered that life would be quiet and easy-going from now on. The men were going to serve out their time and there would be no more trouble. But some warders, notably the hardliners, did not jump at this marvellous opportunity. They thought that any sort of co-operation with the Provos was a bad idea. When the prisoners who were co-operating managed to get these warders confined, the ranks of the warders were split in two. With the threat of violence hanging over the prison, the prison authorities backed down and relegated the hardliners to out-of-the-way places. This co-operation paid off. The Provos got their men into key orderly positions, and they got movement throughout various Blocks. They could build on that. Prisoners and warders were on first-name terms. One particular prison officer would come down to H-Block 7. He had behaved badly during the hunger strikes and was hated with a vengeance. He jumped at the chance for peace in his time. He came onto the Block often, and acted as if he was one of the prisoners. His flamboyant attitude was resented deeply, but the Provos held their tongues. He liked to think he had his ear close to the ground and went out of his way to be friendly to prisoners, especially to Bik McFarlane. And McFarlane went out of his way to make him feel welcome. McFarlane was very polite, always saying 'please' and 'thank you'. His attitude stuck in the throats of some of his fellow inmates. They thought he was carrying co-operation a little too far. But it paid off. McFarlane was able to name who he wanted transferred to his Block. Conspiracies began to develop between warders and prisoners. Cell 26 was the orderly cell on each Wing, and was a double cell. By prison directive there were supposed to be no more than three men in Cell 26 at any one time. It was used frequently by prisoners for meetings and lectures and briefings, and there were frequently a dozen men in Cell 26. If a senior prison officer was coming the warders would rush in and tell the prisoners to scatter. They would leave and behave like model prisoners for the duration of the visit, and then they would turn to the warders. Don't worry, they said, we won't drop you in it—we won't tell the Governor that you allowed a dozen of us to use Cell 26. The warders would feel quite relieved that the prisoners were acting fairly, they would end up feeling grateful to the prisoners. It was an ironic twist.

The prison authorities were forced to appoint more orderlies than necessary. There wasn't enough work to go around, nor orderly positions. The effect was that any Provo who wanted to 'work' would have no problem finding a position of some sort. And so the Provos got their own men in the Circle of each Block they were intending to control. They got their men into the kitchen so that other plots could be hatched. They came a long way in a short space of time. Everything in Long Kesh seemed to be running just fine.

And then, coming up to Christmas of 1982, the Provos got a gift. One prisoner had become very friendly with a warder, they had even discussed their personal lives on occasions. Now the prisoner asked the warder to do him a favour. He wanted something in for Christmas, would the warder bring it in for him? There was some hesitation as the warder asked what he wanted. The prisoner wanted a bottle of vodka. No problem, the warder would bring in the bottle of vodka. He brought it in, and was paid £20. But it wasn't the vodka that was important. The willingness of a warder to bring in a drink at Christmas was indicative of something that ran deeper. As far as the warders were concerned, the Provos were playing ball with the prison regime. Other warders did other small favours for other prisoners. The cumulative effect of these favours was to place the prisoners and the warders into seemingly close relationships. From those close relationships would come information which could help the men to break out of Long Kesh.

3

Getting the Blocks Solid

Some men in the Blocks dream a lot to stay sane. There are all sorts of dreams for the men in Long Kesh. And nightmares. Most prisoners are married or have girlfriends on the outside. And when you go in for twenty years, or even worse, at the Secretary of State's Pleasure, life can be grim for those on the outside, as well as those on the inside. For the women married to the men in prison, life can be hell. There is always the waiting time. How long will it be before he gets out? During the years of protest that waiting time was doubled every day that passed. All you could get were visits, sometimes. There are always visits, but no privacy on the visits. There's a 'screw' looking over your shoulder listening to what's being said. And there's the carrying of comms, IRA comms and personal comms. The personal ones are where she tells him her personal thoughts, and he his. They say what both of them are really thinking—sometimes. Written out late the night before, slipped to each other secretly in an intimate moment, passed from mouth to mouth in front of the 'screw' watching. Trying to keep a relationship going is bad, very bad, when you can never have a private word for years on end. Some get divorced. Some try and work something out. But some of the men torture themselves in the Blocks late at night wondering what she's doing now. They are alone in their cell, and just start thinking. Is she seeing someone else? Well, they can understand that. Twenty years is a long time to wait. The men could understand her seeing someone else. And then the thought of her seeing someone else makes them want to climb the walls. So the next visit, they ask her straight out if she's seeing someone else. The warders are there, and the visit turns into an inquisition. And it's spoiled. And that time is gone forever. And there's no way to turn the clock back to the start again. At home,

37

some women turn into Green Cross widows. If they go out with somebody else, they think it will get back to their man inside. Some feel watched all the time. Some are. The visits and secret comms are supposed to keep love alive over the decades. Sometimes even genuine concern by friends and neighbours can seem intrusive and simply appear as an effort to keep tabs on her.

The women carry the comms, their personal ones and the IRA ones. Without the women, there would be little communication between the outside and inside. Carrying IRA comms takes precedence over their own. Wives, sisters, mothers, girlfriends, hold the comms in their mouths. Comms can be swallowed, and will pass through the human digestive system unharmed. They can be retrieved and sent back through the lines again if something goes wrong, if there's a search and you can't be sure that the comm won't be taken. IRA comms are always swallowed if anything goes wrong.

One thing that never leaves the mind in Long Kesh is the dream of escape, always escape. The thoughts of tunnels and ropes and ladders fill long hours. Escape. To get away and spend some private time. Thoughts of escape appear like dreams. But the thoughts of escape are not without foundation. Since 1970 there have been hundreds of escape attempts from prisons in the North, and many never even get as far as being attempted. Successful escapes involving large numbers of prisoners have been few and far between. In the early seventies security in prisons was very lax and the early escapes bore little resemblance to what might be required in the eighties.

The first main one was in June 1971 when Gerry FitzGerald, a 17-year-old Provo from Ballymurphy, tried to get away. He had been shot while trying to blow up a petrol station in Belfast and was lodged in the Royal Victoria Hospital with a bullet hole through his leg. Two RUC men carrying 9mm Walther pistols stood guard. Four men in white coats, and armed with shortarms, entered the hospital. They held up the policemen, relieved them of their weapons, scooped up the patient and left. The last the two policemen saw of FitzGerald were his unsuccessful attempts to cover his buttocks as he was carried away. FitzGerald didn't move too far. He stayed in a house opposite the hospital for a number of weeks before he moved across the border.

After internment was introduced in August 1971 the numbers held in State custody increased dramatically. And with the increase in numbers escape attempts became more frequent, more intense, and in some cases, more bizarre. These attempts were given all the more impetus because IRA men and women felt that what they were doing was right and justified, and that they should not be in jail in the first place, and that therefore they were duty bound to escape, or to keep trying at the very least. Anything they could do to get out was okay.

In 1972 there was a major escape from a prison ship, the *Maidstone*, moored at that time in Belfast Lough, and holding internees. Seven men covered their bodies with grease, lowered themselves into the icy water, swam under the barbed wire and arrived at the shore. They then hijacked a bus and drove into the Markets area of Belfast.

The following year saw a large number of escapes. John Greene walked out of Long Kesh wearing his brother's clothes. His brother was a priest and he was discovered afterwards in the Cage, tied up. Brendan Hughes left Long Kesh by sneaking into a refuse truck. He was dumped under tons of rubbish, some distance from the jail, and he managed to get safely back to Belfast. In 1974 thirty-three men tunnelled their way out of Long Kesh. One escaper, Hugh Coney, was shot dead by the British Army and all the rest were caught almost immediately. And then there was the Newry Courthouse escape the same year, when Papillon and nine others got away through a window.

Following the killing of Coney, the IRSP prisoners in Long Kesh set up a special Escape Committee. It was separate from the Provos and the idea was to coordinate all escape efforts. There was a steel fence surrounding the Camp, and then there was a twenty-foot-high wall. Throughout the period, tunnels had been the main preoccupation of would-be-escapees, even though tunnelling attempts had been largely unsuccessful. The ground around the Kesh was sandy and ideal for digging. But only one tunnel had even been made without detection, and all thirty-three escapees had been caught almost at once. The prison authorities had sensory equipment buried in the sand all over the camp. A British Army helicopter circled the area every two days, taking x-ray photographs which showed up tunnels.

The IRSP people made a list of what they needed. Their people on the outside got a wire cutters, and cut it up into sections. Alternative sections had threads bored into them and the cutters was smuggled in, one piece at a time, and re-assembled on the inside. Handles for the cutters were made from tubular chair legs. Several chisels were brought in to chip away at the concrete on the floor of the hut where the tunnel was to start. The Camp workshop supplied all the equipment necessary to make a grappling hook for the wall. A blow heater, supplied by the authorities for heating the hut, was used to ventilate the shaft as it was being dug. But it was March 1977 before a decision was taken as to who was going out. Those facing the longest sentences were offered an opportunity to leave. The Belfast IRSP wanted those people who could be most useful out. Useful, that is, in so far as operational capability went.

The digging was carried out by two-man relays, working in shifts, day and night. Floor tiles from the hut were glued to a block and used as a trapdoor for the tunnel. The sand and soil were stored in the men's lockers and between the corrugated walls of the Nissan huts. The tunnel itself was eighteen inches wide to avoid the necessity for using too many support beams. But almost immediately, men hit a seam of concrete. The concrete had been poured into an old Provo tunnel which had been discovered by the authorities. The men dug under it and their tunnel had to be sloped even more to accommodate this change. After another two days' digging, they hit another seam of concrete. In all they met five old tunnels. The place was so full of holes and tunnels it was called 'The Mole Hill'. By the time they passed those five seams they weren't too sure which direction they were heading in but they were pretty sure that they had made it to the other side of the fence. After all, they had spent three solid weeks digging. But the day before the escape was due to go, they discovered a crack running along on the ground outside. They brought forward the escape.

Around 9 pm on 4 May, two men opened the trapdoor and went down. They crawled on their bellies, and when they reached the end of the tunnel they pulled on a string, which they had brought with them. Two more followed. Ten men following in all. And when they came out on the surface, they discovered that they were wrong, they weren't on the far side of the fence. The fifteen foot of steel mesh faced them. Across the way, there was the twenty-foot-high wall. In between, stood a British Army watch tower and amber arc lamps. They cut the wire and dashed across the clearing without being spotted. One man took the grappling hook and threw it as high as he could. It caught first time. As the first man reached the top of the wall, the hook and the rope and the man came tumbling down. His leg was injured and he had to be brought back through the tunnel. The others scrambled across the wall finally, and dropped onto the disused RAF airfield on the far side. There was a botched back-up. There was nobody to meet them, and so the men headed towards the M1 motorway. Two were caught by police eight miles from the camp. The authorities were still unaware that any escape had taken place. The other seven made it across the border.

Throughout the seventies one man who also tried to escape on a countless number of occasions was Gerry Kelly. Kelly had been involved in planting two car bombs in London in March 1973. One was planted at the Old Bailey and the second was at New Scotland Yard. When the bombs went off one man died of a heart attack, and 180 were injured. Nine people were charged and convicted of the offences, including Kelly. Kelly refused to wear prison clothes and lost all privileges. A gruelling hunger strike was undertaken to allow those convicted to serve out their sentences in the North. Force feeding was used in an attempt to break the strike.

Eventually in 1976, Kelly was moved back to the North along with three of his co-accused. He had political status in the Cages but an unsuccessful escape attempt landed him in the Blocks. At one point, he was in Musgrave Park Hospital receiving treatment for a collapsed lung when he tried to get away, but he was spotted by a nurse and that idea fell through. Kelly was a respected Provo and had a major input into the thinking that dominated the movement within the jail leading up to the hunger strike, and afterwards. The Provos could also draw inspiration from more modern escapes as well. And the more recent escapes were from places which bore some resemblance to the security conditions under which they were held in Long Kesh.

It was Wednesday 10 June 1981. It was in the afternoon and solicitors were conferring with their clients in the basement of Crumlin Road Jail. There were eight Provos there, and three of them had murder charges pending against them. They were known as the M60 Squad, by virtue of the fact that the offences with which they were charged were carried out using an M60 heavy machinegun. Prison Officer Richard Kennedy was suddenly confronted by two of the men, one carrying a small pistol. Kennedy hit one of them with his baton when he realised what was happening, but he was knocked to the ground and locked up. The Provos then took the solicitors, the rest of the warders and ordinary criminals. Two Provos put on warders' clothes and a third dressed as a solicitor. They had three gates and 200 yards to go. The warder on the first gate realised that all was not well when the 'solicitor' tried to brush past without having his pass scrutinised properly. At gunpoint the officer was forced to open the gate. Another warder looked out the window in the Administration building and saw a Provo he recognised carrying a baton. He slammed the office door shut and pressed the alarm button. The baton-wielding Provo smashed his way through the glass in the door and all eight ran towards the gate.

Outside the prison, just across the road, was Crumlin Road Courthouse. Three detectives waited in a car for a fourth to emerge from the Courthouse. They saw the IRA men coming through the gates. It looked as if there were warders chasing prisoners and the detectives drove the car towards the men. The eight jumped over a low wall close to the Courthouse, and one of them jumped into a waiting car. The glass was shattered when the detectives started to open fire on the vehicle. The lone IRA man lurched the car into a wall and the detectives decided to go after the other seven. All eight got away. The eight were covered by active service units of the IRA who had been in position beforehand. But some of the escapees were caught in the South, and were jailed for the escape under the Criminal Law Jurisdiction Act. The Act allowed for trial and conviction in the South for offences committed in the North, and was the only left-over of the ill-fated Sunningdale Agreement of the mid-seventies.

Traditionally, escapees were treated as heroes by many people in the South. They went here and there, making public appearances, and giving embellished accounts of the escape. Attempts to have escapees extradited from the South back to the North had failed repeatedly during the seventies. Escape from custody was considered a political offence and exempt from extradition. But in the eighties the atmosphere had changed in the South. Escapees could no longer be sure of a safe haven as far as the government was concerned. Following the convictions of some of the Crumlin Road escapees in the South, the thinking changed within the Provos. The convictions had a profound effect on the sort of lives led by escapees. For example, it was no longer possible to live openly or have any sort of normal life. But if that line of thought was clear to the Provos on the outside, it was far from clear inside Long Kesh. The men dreamed of getting away and getting back into the fight, of at least having some measure of control and freedom over their own lives.

By early 1983 Papillon had the basics worked out. There was still much information that he hadn't got. He was good at gathering people together and getting them to find out specific pieces of information. Nobody had the full picture of what was happening—yet. People were just asked to watch this or that, a watch tower here, the time it took to get from A to B there. Papillon was looking for a weakness in the security of the prison at this point. But security was very tight. And when security is that tight, Papillon knew that the next thing to work on and to exploit was human weakness.

Meanwhile, the final push for segregation was on. The warders were under the impression that the Provos were about to start war with them again. They could hear the rumours going around the Blocks. There were threats against the loyalists, and killing and death were being mentioned very frequently, too frequently for the warders' liking. The warders and the Provos had a meeting. The warders wanted to know if the policy had changed, if there were going to be shootings on the outside. No, there was no change in policy, no warders were going to be killed—as long as the unacceptable warders were kept well away, there would be no trouble. The Provos said that if the unacceptable warders were allowed near them, and they started to rock the boat, their names would be sent to the outside, and they would be dealt with. The Provos started to end the protests in large numbers. They went to the Governor in turn, said they were broken, that they couldn't take it any more. The loyalists were starting to get outnumbered. They went on a no-work protest and were locked up for a week, refusing to come out of their cells. H-Blocks 6, 7 and 8 began to come under Provo control. As the loyalists began to escalate their protests, the

Provos went further and said they wanted to be totally conforming prisoners. This involved doing work and agreeing to live in mixed Wings with the loyalists. The prison administration couldn't cope with the speed at which events were taking place. The Provos were going into the system in unprecedented numbers, and the loyalists were moving out. Suddenly, segregation was achieved in three major Blocks. But forced integration was something the prison authorities could always hold over both sets of prisoners in the jail.

The first weakness Papillon discovered was in the workshops. The searching of men coming and going wasn't that tight. Papillon decided that it was possible to take a workshop. But there was a problem. Workshops were mixed, and the Provos didn't have enough men in any one workshop to be sure of controlling it in the inevitably tense situation which would arise as soon as they made a move. The idea was scuppered, but reappeared from time to time. They checked out the kitchen, to see if it were possible to take it. They checked out the hospital, could they take that? They checked out every building in the camp. They just continued to throw ideas around and gather intelligence on everything. All information was useful.

It was April of that year before a new command staff was elected in Long Kesh. Papillon was Head of the Escape Committee. He was also a Welfare Officer and Intelligence Officer for escapes. He needed to get men into strategic positions, and to get a very clear mental picture of the prison. All movements and security started to be logged by men coming and going to the workshops. The information was kept right up to date. The key workers were people who were known to be reliable, people who had been involved in previous escape attempts and were known as people who could keep a closed mouth. Nobody was told what the information was being gathered for. Some men thought that the information was being gathered to attack the workshops, and finish the no-work issue once and for all. They took the view that going to work was just a strategy, so that the Provos could get inside the workshops, and wreck them, and finish all work for ever.

Papillon had less than two years left to serve when Fig arrived in the prison. The two men started to work together. They began to spend a lot of time together, plotting and planning. There were ground rules. Fig was new into the Blocks, had been active, knew the damage informers had done to the movement on the outside. There were rumours to the effect that the prison authorities were also trying to get people on the inside to turn informer. The first ground rule was that people should not be told anything they didn't need to know. Then if people turned they would have very little to say. And the men couldn't talk amongst themselves about something they knew nothing about. Everything was on a need-to-know basis. Fig and Papillon started to bounce ideas off each other, to teach each other. Papillon taught Fig all the Irish names for the security gates and sensitive points in the camp. They would talk easier that way. If they were overheard by warders, no suspicion would attach to them. 'That gate looks easy to take' in Irish didn't cause one warder's head to turn. Papillon was older, more experienced, had seen more than ten years in jail. Fig was younger, more enthusiastic, more brash. Fig knew all the leaders on the outside, had worked well with them. He was respected. If he told the outside that something was possible, they would back him up. But the ideas that the two men had were still shifting. They knew they could take a Block, they had a lorry, they were gathering information, but still nothing solid. Some of the lifers were getting desperate. They wanted out. They followed the traditional way of looking for the weakest point of security and working on that. Tunnels and ladders were being mentioned. But it was 600 yards to the outside, and that was a very long tunnel indeed. One team who wanted to dig their way out was given the go-ahead.

Papillon decided that it would be a good idea if Fig memorised the layout of the entire camp. That way, if he was moved to another Block, he could take the layout with him in his head. A moveable map. Papillon took Fig right into his own cell.

'Right, Fig,' he said as he turned his picture board, revealing a stretched polythene sheet tacked onto the back of it, 'here goes.' Papillon produced a felt-tipped marker and began to draw.

'Where did you get that stuff?' shouted Fig.

Papillon smiled and shook his head. 'You'll never know. I have contacts everywhere.'

They started off with the Block. It took Fig weeks to memorise the layout, and to be able to draw the map properly. Colour codes were used for different security arrangements. At different times, the two men almost came to blows over the maps, one getting angrier than the other as Fig failed to memorise correctly. All the gates and buildings were codenamed, so that the two could discuss the plan anywhere. Papillon had a sense of humour; he codenamed the Control Room 'Big T', after a Provo on the outside who would later prove crucial.

The food lorry was studied. The time it took to get from one Block to another timed. The lorry moved more or less at random, not starting or finishing the Blocks in any particular order. Papillon wondered if the same driver was used all the time. He wondered if the same prisoner was used as his helper all the time. He wondered if either of the two men would work for him. They needed the help of other Blocks to find these things out. The word came back: the same driver, the same helper, all the time. Things were looking up. The Provos could find no way to pressurise the driver. They wondered if they could buy him off. Papillon decided that it would be better not to approach the driver or helper at all. If they made an approach and either man decided he didn't want to be any part of the escape, he could go to the authorities and the plan would be up in the air. Papillon turned up someone else who was to prove far more helpful. One member of the Escape Committee remembered another friendly face from the hospital during the hunger strike. So they approached the man in the hospital. He'd help them all right. So he gave them information but he didn't tell them anything they didn't already know. Papillon kept updating all the information flowing to him from all ends of the prison. Fig was gathering it and Papillon was collating it, making sense of it, watching for a weakness. The lorry was the key. They knew the time it took to get from one Block to another, its routine before and after it visited the prison. The most important thing they found out about the lorry was that the warders never bothered to check the back of it. The warders were quite sure about their prison, it was one of the most secure in Western Europe. There was little point in checking the lorry on the way out. Nobody could escape.

Papillon planned to take the Control Room, the nerve centre of the entire prison. He was going to use the lorry to get that far. It didn't seem such a problem. He and Fig spent all their waking hours talking escapes, thinking escapes, planning. Papillon said it would be easy to take the lorry. All they needed was a man on the floor of the lorry with a gun trained on the driver. They could get the gun in from the outside. All the driver had to do was to do what he did every day. There would be little risk. The warders would open and close the gates for him and the lorry wouldn't be checked for any extra passengers. Sunday would be a good day to take over. Sundays were lazy days in Long Kesh, there were fewer staff on. But they only had the bones of an escape. There were countless problems to overcome.

They didn't know the security procedures used to get the lorry through the control area. They still had to get weapons in. They didn't know which Block or Blocks to take. They hadn't decided who was going out on the escape, or how many, or what would happen once they got as far as the outside. Fig and Papillon decided that it was time enough to decide who should go, they tried to get a better plan first. Through the summer of 1983 they continued to update their files. A lot of pieces were missing.

There were many ways in which the Provos could fill in those missing pieces. They had their own men coming and going throughout the prison. Visitors could fill in information about the entrance. In casual conversation, they could elicit other details from the warders. A willing warder could fill in other spaces for them. But there was a problem about getting such a warder. And if the Provos made an approach and failed, it could hamper all their plans. But the thought that a warder might be prepared to work for money never left Papillon's mind. Further information was collated as the summer approached. The security arrangements were known, as were the manner of car searches. And which gates were the most troublesome to get through.

The Provos managed to get information on the Main Control Room—what it looked like and where everything was located. They also found out what lay between the Control Room and the front gate. The fact that warders passed on some of the information unwittingly was not surprising. It wasn't unusual to see Provos and warders chatting to each other. This was especially true of the OCs of the various wings and Blocks. The Provos managed to get the security arrangements, the codes that were used to move out of the prison, the procedures to be followed.

On their diagrams and maps, the locations of all the alarm buttons were dotted in as soon as they were known. There were different types of alarms. There were some which didn't work.

The Provos began to find out which ones worked and which ones didn't. In the event of a warder pressing a dud alarm button in the middle of an escape attempt, it would save a life if they knew it wasn't going to go off. The Provos had a camera and they managed to photograph the entire route that the food lorry took each day. It wasn't done all at once. It was done one piece at a time and then the route was put together. It was easy for the Provos to take photographs of various parts of the prison. Some of the time, they moved from the workshops in groups and it was possible to conceal the camera. The Provos managed to get a lot but they didn't get everything.

Fig and Papillon stayed awake at night wondering how they could get the weapons into the jail. Warders were being searched, and they didn't think it was possible to get them in that way. Warders were being searched, not because they were considered security risks, but because food and materials were disappearing from the prison at an unprecedented rate. Spot checks were sometimes carried out and the two men thought it very risky to try and get weapons in like that. But then other problems started to arise. The men in the garden had come up with a plan to get away. Now they came to the Escape Committee, composed of about five men, all senior Provos, and asked for clearance. The five men talked it over. If the garden men went, and failed, it would be bad for morale; if they went, and succeeded, it might interfere with the larger escape. It was decided to let the men go ahead with their plans—for the moment, but they watched the situation closely. There were also other escapes in the pipeline. Different groups of men were going to the Committee and looking for clearance for different types of escapes. They were given the go-ahead, but they were also being stalled. They had no idea why. Some were very unhappy about this, and complained that the new Committee wasn't working and they wanted to return to the old command structures and planning methods. The new Committee had only just started, they were told, give it a chance. As far as the prison authorities and warders were concerned, the Provos were buckling down to serve their sentences. There were still some men on protest, diehards who might never end it. Life seemed a little easier, a very welcome development. For years the warders had been at war with the Provos. Many had been shot dead, fingered from the inside. Many had personal problems as a result of the stresses and tensions that went with the job. They were relatively well paid. But marriages had fallen apart, more had a drink problem, some gambled heavily. They were doing a job for a wage, and they were pitted against men who had very little money or possessions and who carried forward a war as a result of their political beliefs. Many warders worked their normal forty-hour week, and then thirty hours overtime on top of that. There was a shortage despite the fact that their numbers had increased greatly since the early seventies. A thousand warders looked after the prisoners. It is easy to see how they could be lulled into a false sense of security when the Provos started to co-operate with them and to make life easier. With Provo co-operation, the Blocks ran smoothly, incidents decreased, there was give and take. The warders went along with this just to get the job done. The Provos did it to get control, to place their men where they wanted them, to escape.

Papillon was faced with the following. There was a 2,000-yard wall taking in more than an eighty-acre complex. There were about 500 Provos, and 150 of them had taken up positions as orderlies in an many parts of the prison as they could gain access to. Information was flowing from all directions. There was a steel grille which controlled all movement in and out of each Block. The bar on the H of each Block contained the Circle and the entrance to the Block. That entrance had a double-gated vehicle lock. That would have to be taken. The Communications Room was in the Circle. There were alarms and telephones there and there were two locked doors to get through. That would have to be knocked out. Each Block had a sixteen-foot-high fence. If the plan was to take all the Blocks, the problems were multiplied by eight. The entire prison was divided into segments which were cut off by concrete walls and wire fences. There were no more than three Blocks in a segment. There were television monitors and alarms all over the place, and a seventeen-foot-high wall enclosed the entire complex. And there was a wire fence surrounding the wall, made up of razor wire and spread out low along the ground. Spaced every 200 yards around the prison there was a watch tower which overlooked all activity, and the the twelve towers held British soldiers. There were two double gates in the fence, called the outer fence, which controlled all vehicle and pedestrian access to the prison. This was the External gate. The Prison Guard Force, ready to move once the alarm went off, was outside the wall, but inside the fence. The watch tower men were drawn from here. They also patrolled the outside.

There were a lot of men dreaming in Long Kesh of getting out, dreaming of spending time with their wives and girlfriends. They had spent years in the Blocks and weren't likely to get out before the end of the century. Only Papillon had a plan for getting some of them out. The plan was far from ready, but it was a plan which could work. Papillon knew that the trouble with tunnel and ladders was that they weren't going to work, the ideas were old. The time could come when those lifers who were planning escapes by those routes might have to be ordered to knock them on the head. But not yet. As the summer of 1983 came, it was too early to stop them.

4

The Plan

By the summer of 1983, the Provos were very strong in H7. There were already many lifers in that Block, and they had good control. Any changes which the prison authorities wanted to implement had to go through the men first. The running battles over segregation and unacceptable warders were still fresh in everyone's mind. For no apparent reason incidents between warders and prisoners took a nosedive in H7 that summer. The real reason was quite simple: the prisoners in H7 were under orders from their officers not to cause any trouble.

One directive went out from the Governor's office. It was a petty directive and stated that no cell should have more than one picture board if there was only one man in the cell. Each prisoner was allocated a board, to pin up pictures and notes. Where there were two men in a cell, there were two boards. Under normal circumstances there would be a major row over attempts to restrict something like picture boards; as a matter of principle, the men would have refused to conform. The orders were sent to the men but there was no trouble, and they gave up the boards peacefully. Some of the prisoners didn't like the order and through their leaders were going soft, but even more confusing to many of them was the behaviour of Bik McFarlane.

He seemed to spend his days wandering all over H7 as an orderly, going out into the yard, cleaning his way throughout the Block, and going out of his way to be polite to warders. He would smile and laugh and joke with them. He seemed interested in their lives. McFarlane was incapable of being false, and even if he was ordered to be friendly with someone in order to get information out of them, it would be difficult for him. He had no problems being nice in order to cool the temperature of the Block, though. He seemed to be bending over backwards to ingratiate himself with the prison authorities, and on more than one occasion, some of the men felt like tackling him. His record over the hunger strike period was impeccable, but he seemed to have gone soft in the head.

Papillon, meanwhile, had made some decisions. It was possible to take H7 and H8. The idea to take the entire prison had been scrapped as being unfeasible, and H7 and H8 were now the targets. It was possible to take both Blocks and move all the men out. H7 was already very strong in IRA terms. The plans for taking the Block were already there, and it wasn't a problem. But he was by now starting to have trouble with other would-be-escapees.

Men in the concrete yard had come up with a plan. They looked for clearance from the Escape Committee, but they were told to hold on for a while. They came back with the plans again. They were knocked back, and they wanted to know why they were not being allowed to proceed. They couldn't be told the truth. If they went ahead with their plans, and they failed, the repercussions would reverberate throughout the Blocks. Security in the Blocks had never been tested. The first escape would have to work. The men in the concrete yard and elsewhere, who were all planning to leave the prison by various circuitous routes, felt they were being cheated. And while they weren't being told lies, they were not being told the full truth either. Some of the men began to suspect that there was something big afoot but couldn't pin it down. What was heart-breaking for those men was the realisation that there was something happening but that they weren't a part of it.

Papillon and Fig and three others were still collecting and collating all their information on movements and security checks within the prison. The prison was now viewed in stages. The first stage was the Block, the second was the Segment and the third was the way out. They visualised the security as three rings, one outside the other. They had no idea how to get through the last phase—the main gate. Up to that point they knew that passwords, or passcards, were used to get cars through.

It was a throwaway question one day. A prisoner was chatting to a warder, just general talk about the warder going off duty, and how long it might take him to get home, considering all the security checks, and how long it took to get out the last gate. The last gate wouldn't delay him, he said, there was only a playing card used there. A playing card. An ordinary playing card. They were handed in on the way in and returned on the way out. They couldn't believe it, a deck of playing cards would get them out of the last gate.

The prisoners continued to get closer and closer to the warders. As the relationships became more and more personal, Provo intelligence files began to grow. Even information not useful to the escape was being collected, collated, filed away. Warders might talk about where they went for a drink, who they went with. The information could come in handy some day. The warders got so friendly with Bik McFarlane that they forget how dangerous he really was and what he was capable of. It was the same for the rest of the orderlies. Orderlies who worked H7 had a fairly easy time. There was Bik McFarlane, and Bobby Storey, Brendan Mead, Sean McGlinchey, Gerry Kelly, Tony McAllister. They were out of their cells for most of the day. Some pushed food trolleys, some cleaning machines, some were medical orderlies. They were out and about between 8.30 and 9.30 every morning. The most senior men within the Provos, along with the five on the Escape Committee, had an input into the escape plans. They had to. They were going to have to carry them out.

Orderlies were supposed to be locked up for an hour at that point in the forenoon. Usually they weren't. After exercise, which took place outside if the weather was favourable, there was lock-up for an hour, between 1 and 2. They were usually left wandering about then as well. There was really very little need to lock them up, everything was going smoothly. Everyone was on the same side. They might hold a class in politics or Irish. Nobody objected if there were only three or four men there.

Only key people had an idea about the plan to take the two Blocks. Most of those who knew most about the plans were in other Blocks, planning and plotting to secure the release of other men. One crucial factor in the escape was that it had to be sold to the Army Council of the IRA on the outside. Without their help and support the entire exercise was a waste of time. The plans had to be drawn up in a clear and articulate manner. Papillon was linked into the outside through Fig. The IRA nominated one person from the Army Council, one from the Northern

Command and one from General Headquarters Staff, to deal with the plans for the escape. The men on the inside were sure by that summer that they would need weapons to take the Blocks. The men on the inside linked up with the Belfast Brigade to get the necessary weapons.

Other Brigade areas throughout the North were asked to come up with small weapons—weapons that could be smuggled easily, that could be hidden. Small guns, .25s, known as 'ladies weapons' would be ideal. The IRA searched through its arsenals to get the guns. Communication between the men on the inside and the Provos on the outside was easy. Comms were sent in through wives, girlfriends, mothers, sisters. They were passed to the men, who went to the workshops and fed them back to the right Blocks. It was a complex system, but it rarely failed. A prisoner could send a comm to a workshop, get it brought out, delivered, and an answer back by a similar route—all on the same day. One person on the outside dealt with all the comms from the men planning the escape.

The men who worked in the workshops were used to carry messages from one Block to another. Comms were passed during working hours, and freedom of movement meant that access was easy. Warders were aware that comms were being exchanged all the time, but it wasn't worth doing anything about it. After all, many of the Provos were lifers and had nothing to lose by putting up a fight over a comm. It made little material difference to the time a lifer spent in prison to end up on the Boards for a while after hitting a warder. There were other places as well where comms were passed from prisoner to prisoner, from Block to Block. There was the football pitch of H7 where orderlies could meet up and compare notes on how plans were progressing. It was possible for cleaning orderlies to be at the warders' huts, and then to wander over to the football pitch casually. The prison hospital was another area which allowed messages to pass unhindered between the men.

There was a gap of about 300 yards between the metal fabrication shop and the concrete yard. Men working in the concrete yard had to wear steel-tipped boots for protection. Those steel tips could only be got in the metal fab shop, located in old aircraft hangars. One hangar was a store and there were piles and piles of plastic chairs all over the place. Frames for tables and chairs were scattered around. There was a small office located in the corner. The rest of the hangars contained work benches with machinery for pressing and cutting metal. It was easy for Papillon and other members of the Escape Committee to meet and talk in the metal workshop. Warders didn't mind. They could stay there for fifteen or twenty minutes, while another orderly made a cup of tea for the warders. The warders thought nothing of this, it was normal.

It was late June by the time the final plans were ready. The detailed plans were written out on fifty sheets of toilet paper. These were the plans to take H7. It was decided to drop the idea of taking other Blocks, there were enough problems in holding just one Block. The strategy changed from taking two Blocks to taking one Block and getting as many people as the Provos wanted into that Block in time for the escape.

Papillon handed the plans over to his number two, and further details about dates were added. Those plans were then presented to the Army Council on the outside. When the outside had first been contacted about the escape, their reaction had been simple: they told the men they were crazy, there was no way out of the Blocks, everyone knew that.

But gradually, through the involvement of trusted people, they came to change their minds, and said they would back any plan that had a realistic chance of success. The plan that Papillon presented to his number two had a good chance of success. The plan was very simple: they would take control of H7, hijack the food lorry and drive out of the camp. Papillon had all the men he needed in more or less the right places to carry the escape through. He counted up how many weapons he was going to need: six. The outside would have to find six small weapons. All the orderlies were in position in H7, they were all reliable, they were all lifers. In H7 there were constant briefings and discussions. They nearly always used Cell 26, the double cell. In spite of the directive which stated that no more than three prisoners should use it at any one time, it was hard for a warder to refuse them when they came up to him with a cup of tea and said they were going into Cell 26 for a while and to give them a rap on the door if there was a Governor coming down to the Block. There was one time when the warders tried to implement that directive. It ended up that there were fifteen or sixteen men shouting at the top of their voices at them. That was just one step away from major trouble. Cell 26 became very important in the last few months leading up to the escape date. It was necessary for key people to have a place to meet and discuss developments.

It was early July when the Army Council sanctioned the escape plans. They were happy enough with what was proposed. The three-person committee was now in charge of dealing with the details. They set up another committee, made up of people from the Belfast Brigade and the South Armagh Brigade. These two Brigades were responsible for finding the necessary weapons to get into the prison, and to make sure the back-up was there when and if the men got out. But the men on the inside still had options. They would drive away from the prison in the lorry. Or they could split up as soon as they got outside the gate and use cars—prison officers' cars which were conveniently parked nearby. At the end of the day they decided on a combination of these two options. They would drive as far as the main gate, some Provos would be left at the gate while the lorry made its getaway, and the remaining men would get away in warders' cars. It seemed a simple plan.

The Provos on the outside started to plan too. They said they would provide back-up. They would come to within ten miles of the prison on the day of the escape. They would have fifty heavily armed men and women waiting. The escapees would reach the pick-up point, at least three quarters of them would be armed immediately, and the combined force, now numbering 100, would move back southwards towards South Armagh. South Armagh was a good place to head for because there were no British soldiers on the ground. There were British soldiers in the area, but their movements were confined. The only way they could get in and out safely was to use helicopters, and they had made certain bases in South Armagh the busiest heliports in Europe. When the unit of about 100 people travelled back into South Armagh, their backs would be covered by at least another half dozen units of the IRA. The road back into South Armagh would be mined in at least three places. Then, if the escapees were followed, IRA men and women would allow those chasing them to get as far as the third mine before blowing up the road. All the units would be in constant radio contact with each other. If there were more British Army or RUC still following the escapees, they would know about it. Then the second mine would be blown. The last mine to be exploded would be closest the prison. The units had their own plans to make their getaway. Safe houses had been arranged for the escapees. It was a mammoth operation, which drew heavily on the resources of the IRA. The organisation of the pick-up and back-up would take considerable time, but they had lots of that at this stage. Everything would be taken care of as soon as they reached the pick-up point, just ten miles from the prison. Everything depended on the escapees making it to that point.

Both the Belfast Brigade and the South Armagh Brigade promised to set up other diversions to occupy the RUC, UDR and British Army, to keep them busy with other things on the day of the escape itself. This would stretch the resources of the security forces. Again, people were only told things on a need-to-know basis. Even though there were more than 100 involved on the outside, very few were actually told what was happening. The day would be soon enough to tell them. Papillon was happy enough with the plans for the back-up. Everybody was assured that it would be there. Papillon had kept a copy of the fifty sheets of toilet paper with the plans on them. In his cell, he pored over them every now and then, checking details here and there. It looked good. The plans would have to be taken over to H7 somehow. Now all they needed were the weapons. Without the guns, there could be no taking H-Block 7, no food lorry, no escape. But there was a range of ways they could be brought in. The guns themselves were fairly small affairs—five inches by three and a half inches, weighing between eight and ten ozs each. They all could be broken into their component parts. The edges of all five weapons were smoothed, so it was easy to carry them on or *in* the person. The men needed six, but they could only get five, and then they made a replica which looked very like the real thing. One of those five weapons had been used in the Crumlin Road jailbreak in 1981 and hadn't been used by the Provos since.

There were supply lorries coming into the prison all the time. The supplies were unloaded outside the main gate but were not searched very well. Then the supplies were sometimes left for long periods. This meant that it was easy to place a weapon inside the supplies and retrieve it as soon as they were inside the prison. And in the case of building supplies, they weren't checked at all. The concrete yard was an easy place to retrieve and hide a weapon. When food supplies arrived in the kitchen there was

57

hardly any checking done. It was also possible to hide weapons in the laundry, it was hardly ever checked. From either the kitchen or the laundry, the guns could be moved into any of the Blocks. Hundreds of vehicles came into the prison and it was possible to bring weapons in in any one of them. The vans used to bring visitors to the visiting rooms were rarely checked. The policy of co-operation with the warders had relaxed the atmosphere around the prison. As well, visitors could possibly bring the weapons in. There were 800 prisoners in the prison and each was entitled to one visit a week. At any one visit, a prisoner could have three visitors. In theory, 2,400 visitors could visit the prison every week. The authorities could not search everybody, to eliminate totally the possibility of one of them bringing in a weapon.

Visitors were seated in a room which had twenty tables. Five-foot-high partitions between the prisoners gave them semi-privacy. There was another visiting area which had twelve rooms which were intended for discussions between prisoners and lawyers, or prisoners and clergymen. The doors on these visiting areas had panes of glass. But the practice had grown up whereby a prisoner could get a special family visit in one of these rooms. Nothing wrong with that, everything was running smoothly at the prison. Except that it was against regulations.

In the two months prior to the date set for the escape, thirty-seven men from H-Block 7 got fifty-two such special visits. It was possible to have sex during a visit. There was no metal detector used on visitors. Neither were the prisoners scanned with a metal detector after visits. And there were staff in the prison through which the weapons could be brought in. The searching procedure was very lax. There were random searches, but very rarely. Baggage wasn't checked. At peak times, there were 700 members of staff coming on duty at the prison, it was impossible to search them all. The weapons, and the ammunition for those weapons, could be brought in via this route.

There was no shortage of ways of getting the equipment in. The only criterion was that the stuff should get in, and get in safely and quickly. Papillon and Fig wondered how they could get all the plans over to H7 where they were needed. Once the plans were delivered it would be up to H7 to pull all the men together in the necessary positions to take the Block successfully. Fig and Papillon were almost finished with the escape. They had planned it down to the last detail. When the plans got as far as H7, their role would be ended. Their job had to make the escape possible, the men in H7 would have to carry it through.

The plans and photographs were rolled into a rubber bullet shape. There were maps and routes, times and security codes, photographs of the route—everything H7 needed to know. The rubber bullet was covered in cling film. A prisoner who was going on the escape slipped the bullet up his back passage and carried it right into the Block. He was transferred specifically for the escape. Others were also; some men were transferred to H7 and they had no idea that they were even going on an escape.

The leaders of the escape waited for the weapons to arrive. On one hot day in August, the door of a cell was opened. Two weapons were dropped onto the bed—they were small .25s. The door slammed shut and the prisoner departed without saying a word. 'Jesus Christ', shouted one of the prisoners in the cell, 'This isn't the time for the screws to raid us.' The other man started to laugh and he picked up the weapons. He went to the Quartermaster of the Block. 'Can you dump these?' he asked. He showed the man the weapons. The quartermaster nearly lost his mind. He had no hiding place for the weapons, he had never been asked to mind weapons in the Blocks before. He had no idea what was happening. 'Where did you get these?', he asked. There was no reply.

So the Quartermaster had to look after the guns until they were needed. He found a hiding place for them. But still a route had to be found, from H3 to H7. And there were still another three weapons due to come into the jail. It was the end of August. The date had been set for the escape: it would go in mid-September. It would go on the day of the All Ireland Football Final. It would go on Sunday 18 September.

On that day the Provos would carry out the largest operation in their history. The escape would be a morale booster, a propaganda exercise and would put some of their most capable men back into circulation. And that was the last question that needed to be answered. Who was going out? The lorry couldn't take any more than forty men. In H7 there were 125 men in the Block. There was going to be some bad feeling on the day when the takeover took place, when some men would realise that they had no part in the escape, that they were going to be left behind.

5

The Happy Wagon

The food lorry was known as the Happy Wagon among those who planned to drive out of the jail in it. By late August discussion was still continuing about who was going. The IRA on the outside wanted certain people out, they wanted people who could be relied upon to return to active service, or at least take an active part in the movement. There was the added criterion that nobody with less than twelve years left to serve would go out, unless there were further charges pending against them. The reason for this was simple. The risk attaching to getting caught had to be weighed against the remainder of a sentence any one man had left to serve. On the other hand, the Provos on the outside wanted men out who had spent the shortest time in prison, and were still relatively fresh. They would be far more familiar with life on the outside than men who had spent a decade in jail. Lifers were given the option of going, unless they had informed while under interrogation. The proposed list went backwards and forwards between the outside and the prison.

There were exceptions to the lifer rule. For example, there were some men who expected to be either framed or shot dead by the RUC or British Army as soon as they got out. The possibility of getting shot was very real as far as many men were concerned. They only had to think of the incidents in and around Armagh in late 1982 to convince themselves that any risks attending to escaping were minor compared with what awaited them on their release. It seemed pointless waiting around. A decision was taken to take some of those men out. One man was asked if he would consider going on an escape, and he replied that if a helicopter came down in the yard, he would be more than willing to get aboard. He added that he would take part in any foolproof plan. He still didn't know what that plan was.

There were between twenty and thirty lifers already in H7. All that remained was to get other men who were being considered for the escape as far as that block. Many men, even at this stage, still had no idea that there was an escape planned, or even if they had some inkling that something was happening, they had no idea that it was going from H7. If word got out that an escape was planned from H7 there would be hundreds of applications from around the Blocks to get there.

The list got closer and closer to finalisation. Men were being picked for the escape who hadn't a clue what lay in store for them. Jimmy Burns, for example. He was thirty-four and from West Belfast and was serving a recommended minimum of thirty years. He was well known among the men as a person who would write poetry for every occasion. He never stopped writing the stuff, there were poems about his wife, his family, flowers and anything else he could think of. His friends didn't think much of his poetry, but he kept writing it anyway.

Then there was thirty-year-old Paul Brennan from Ballymurphy. He had served six years of a sixteen-year sentence. He was a former internee and had witnessed the burning of Long Kesh in October 1974. The men had called him Dutch for a while, but it was a nickname that didn't stick. Nicknames were supposed to be as derogatory as possible. Brennan got his after a priest at Mass informed his captive audience that he had just returned from Holland, and well, the thing that struck him most of all was that the Dutch were, well, a very ugly people. Just like that. The men christened Brennan Dutch immediately. He was a small stocky man who had a ferocious appetite. Dutch would be taking the Happy Wagon.

Gerard McDonnell was thirty-two from the Falls Road. In March 1978 he had been sentenced to sixteen years for possession of bomb-making materials. He had gone on protest. One prisoner spent two years in the cell next to McDonnell and had no idea what he looked like. All he could hear was the voice. Blute, as he was known, was very forthright in his views. If he heard bad language, he would shout for people to stop cursing. If the men were telling blue jokes he would try and knock that on the head too. His voice would boom down the Wing, 'Hey you, cut that out.' He was very hard on himself both mentally and physically and set very high standards for himself; he also expected everyone else to live up to them. This expectation was greeted by a less than enthusiastic response. Those who spent time in jail with him readily admit that they never met a man who was so unafraid of anything. McDonnell was remembered during the protests. If something nasty was about to happen, if the warders were about to move in and try to do some forced washing or shaving or bathing, McDonnell wouldn't wait for the fight to develop. As soon as the door of the cell was opened he attacked the warders. He didn't think it worthwhile to wait for the warders to start the fight. During the attempts to get segregation orders were coming down all the time. In Wings where the Provos were in a minority the carrying-out of those orders could mean a beating from loyalists. The Wing OC refused to give a certain order which had the possibility of starting trouble. Rows started over whether or not the OC was going to give the order. 'I'll give the order' shouted McDonnell. He was a stubborn man and one of the last six men in H7 on protest when everybody else was finished. The six stuck to their protest, it was all they had left and the decision to end it was very hard for them. McDonnell eventually ended it to take part in the escape. He had an important part in the takeover of the Block.

Paul Kane was twenty-eight and from Ardoyne. He was in for eighteen years for attempted murder and possession. He had been convicted solely on the word of informer Christopher Black. James Donnelly was twenty-one, from the same area, and was also serving time on Black's word. He got 208 years, including fifteen for conspiracy to murder. Kevin Barry Artt was also in on Black's word. He was alleged to have been involved in the killing of Long Kesh Assistant Governor Albert Miles in 1978. All three were going out. Most people were told nothing unless they had a role in the takeover of the Block. A number of people were briefed who would not be going on the escape, and their role was also important in securing the Block until the lorry was well clear. One man wasn't told he was going out until two hours before the escape.

Robert Russell was from West Belfast, aged twenty-five and serving twenty years for attempted murder. He always insisted that he had been framed on the charge and he sometimes got a bit depressed in jail. He had the reputation of being very fond of women, and the lack of any women in Long Kesh only added to his troubles. He was called Goose by the men inside. He had been on remand in Crumlin Road Jail in 1981 when the M60 squad had shot their way out and had been due to go with them. But he was taken ill with pleurisy and rushed to Musgrave Park Hospital and the M60 gang left jail without him. Once Papillon and Fig decided that the escape was going from H7 they decided that Russell would have to get there. He was in another Block and they had no idea how they could get him transferred. Most of the men were transferred as a result of favours to orderlies in H7. Russell had ten days to get to H7 before the escape went.

Papillon and Fig were walking around the yard, wondering how they could get Russell away. Suddenly, Papillon stopped dead, left his friend standing there and went over to a warder. He needed to see a medical orderly, he said, he wasn't feeling too well. The warder took Papillon across the Circle of Russell's Block. Just as both men passed the Governor's office, Papillon took a sharp right and left the warder walking on. The warder followed him into the office. 'I want to speak to you in private,' he said. The warder left the office, annoyed at being brushed aside. 'Governor,' said Papillon, 'you have a bit of a problem in the Wing.'

The man behind the desk was in the dark. 'We have?' he asked. He sat up with his ear cocked.

'Yes, there's a problem in the wing all right,', continued Papillon, 'this man Russell is very hard to control. He's very dangerous.' Papillon outlined a serious problem that had developed with Russell on the Wing. There was the possibility that there could be violence, even death. That wouldn't look good for the man sitting behind the desk who could see his promotion going down the drain. What could be done about this?

Papillon appeared to think for a moment. The solution to the problem would have to come from the man behind the desk. With a little verbal nudging the man behind the desk came up with the idea of moving Russell.

He was also nudged towards sending Russell into H7 where the possibility of violence and death would be eliminated. After a few minutes with Papillon he had come up with a solution to a problem he didn't even realise he had until it had been brought to his attention. Within a couple of days Russell was in H7. Time was slipping by.

Kieran Fleming was another man that was going out. He was twenty-three and from Derry. He had been arrested when he was sixteen years old, along with four others, and charged with the murder of RUC woman Linda Baggley in 1976. He was convicted and was imprisoned indefinitely. The judge, when passing sentence, said that he accepted that none of the accused had fired the fatal shot but he was convinced that they had something to do with it.

Seamus McElwaine would also be a very useful man for the Provos to have out. He was twenty-two, and from Scotstown in County Monaghan. He was convicted for killing a UDR man and an RUC reservist in 1980. While awaiting trial at Crumlin Road Courthouse he had stood as a general election candidate in elections for the Dáil and had received almost 4,000 first preference votes. He was very popular in his native county and was considered to be a good IRA operator.

Among those who began to sniff escape in the air, the talk started. Those who could find out what was happening began to discover things. They noted the movement of men into H7, noted the regime that was being operated, noted that they weren't involved. Accusations started to be made that the Belfast Brigade was trying to get all its own men out at the expense of the country areas. There was some truth in the accusation; of the forty on the provisional list, twenty-five were from Belfast, while there were only three from Derry, two from Donegal, and the rest were from country areas across the North. But if most of those were from Belfast, the Provos had taken a battering in that city. In 1981 large numbers of Provos were caught on operations with weapons and explosives in Belfast. Then there followed a spate of informers. By 1983 most of those who had been caught or named two years earlier were serving their sentences.

While the details of who was going out were being finalised there was another problem for Papillon. The weapons had to be stored in another Block. All five weapons had by now arrived, and were to be held until an opportunity presented itself, or could be made, to move them to H7. Some of them were covered in plasterer's tape and dumped in waterlogged pools of water in washrooms. The men didn't think the warders would find them there. They rarely mopped up the water. Others were hidden in scooped-out floors. More ended up being hidden in the pillars of the doors.

64

But as the day for the escape drew closer there was a change of plan. The original idea had been to leave on Sunday 18 September—All Ireland Football Final Day. That date was changed because on that day there would be heavy security along the border checking cars coming and going to the match in Croke Park in Dublin. The extra security would present extra problems for escapees trying to get across the border. Now the date was set for one week later, Sunday 25 September.

6

Lean Comes Clean

Papillon arrived at the metal fabrication workship. Things weren't too good. He carried a chair to the centre of the floor, and another man from the Escape Committee joined him, while the warder went off for a cup of tea. The two men stayed there for twenty minutes talking. They were finalising the plans and the details. There were also problems.

There were the men in the garden who were planning their own escape. The two men had been in H7 and they would have been due to go on the escape, but they didn't know it. However, they displayed a hitherto hidden interest in gardening. They wanted to work in the hothouses, and grow plants and flowers and fruits. Their real intention had more to do with grappling hooks and ropes than gardening. But if they wanted to do gardening, they would be moved to H1 and they would miss the escape. In the summer there had been discussion about telling them to hold on but it was decided not to tell them. While they would be a loss, and a major one, they didn't need to know. All lifers were offered the opportunity to go, and these two would have been offered the chance when the time came. After pushing for weeks, they were finally moved.

The two lifers had started their gardening, and put a plan together. Their plans for scaling the wall were knocked back in July and August and by early September by were ready to roll. They asked permission to go out. They were refused. They wanted to know why, and the reasons were less than convincing. The two men in the metal fab shop talked about how the two gardeners could be stalled. It was possible to order them not to escape, but there was a chance that they would go anyway. They might decide to move, despite being ordered to stay where they were. They were told that they would be disciplined if they reached the outside. The Army Council wrote to them and ordered them to halt their plans. The two lifers were bewildered. They asked if there was an escaped planned, if a helicopter was going to land in the yard, if it was going to be a big escape. The only thing they were sure of was that there was an escape, and that they were not on it. It broke their hearts. The two had decided to cut the wire first. It was quite ironic that they had planned to cut the wire out of the Cages in exactly the same place as Bik McFarlane, Pat McGeown and Papillon had cut it years and years before when they were trying to get away. But if there was a possibility that the two lifers could screw up the big escape, the Escape Committee simply did not believe that it was possible to cut the wire, scale the wall and escape. The two escapes would not materially affect each other. But the small escape was a distraction that could be done without in those early days in September.

Papillon was saddened by the fact that he was going to stay behind. 'Five years ago I could have gone on this. Now the best escape ever is taking place and I won't be on it.' It was a standing joke among the people who knew what was happening that Papillon would feel resentful at having to leave legally by the front gate when the time came for his release. He would consider that the only honourable way to leave Long Kesh was over the wall, or through a tunnel, or in a food lorry. But there were other problems.

The two men talked about Robert Lean, the latest in a long line of RUC informers. Papillon was assured that Lean could have no effect on the escape, that everything was still on target. While the assurances were welcome, there was always a doubt. Lean was part of a process that had begun almost two years earlier. The Provos, committed to a war of attrition with the British Army and the RUC and UDR, knew that attrition was a two-way street. But if Lean was the latest part of that attrition, it was not the first coming in their direction. It had all started with Christopher Black.

Around 6 pm on 21 November 1981 the Provos set up a road-block in Ardoyne at Brompton Park. Christopher Black and James and Kevin Donnelly were involved. The three men carried three rifles—a Garrand, a 22.50 and a .306. They also had two .32s and a .45. Black wasn't feeling too good, he had drunk the best part of a bottle of vodka the night before and had a hangover. And the feel of the entire roadblock was absolutely wrong for all three men on it.

The Unionist politician, the Rev. Robert Bradford, had been shot dead by the Provos a few days earlier and loyalist retaliatory action was expected. Bradford had been a target for some time; he had asked his supporters to pray that typhoid would break out in Long Kesh during the hunger strikes, he said that would solve the issue. Ardoyne could expect to bear the brunt of any reprisals. The roadblock was an attempt to show the loyal population that the Provos were doing something to stop potential assassins. But it was largely illusory. The three men stayed on the roadblock for about fifteen or twenty minutes. They stopped cars, asked drivers for identification and let them through. The last car they let through was a Department of the Environment lorry, driven by a Protestant. The roadblock was a propaganda exercise. The two Donnelly brothers went home, and around 7 pm the three men met up again. Their plan was to visit the Bone area and to go around all the drinking clubs and to spread the word about the roadblock. They were heading towards the Glenpark Club when the RUC shouted at them to stop. Black took off. The two Donnelly brothers dumped their masks. They were all arrested and taken to Castlereagh Interrogation Centre, where the two brothers and Black were put in cells next to one another. After two days, Black asked the Donnellys if they were talking to the police. No, they weren't talking to the police. Black said he was. Donnelly thought he was joking. On the third day the two brothers were taken out and charged with IRA membership and possession of weapons. In dawn swoops carried out by the RUC thirty-eight more people were arrested. The only evidence against any of them was the word of Christopher Black.

Black had joined the Provos in 1975 and was caught for armed robbery almost immediately. He got ten years and was released in December 1980. On the day of his arrest with the Donnellys he was twenty-eight years old, less than one year at liberty, married with four children. He had stayed quiet for two days. Then he started to ask the police what they could give him if he fingered a few people. 'If I help yous, will yous help me?' he enquired. By now, Black's solicitor had been denied access to his client. Another solicitor took over the brief. It emerged that Black could be helped. He was granted immunity from prosecution. Christopher Black started to talk.

All his statements concerned the summer of 1981, the height of the hunger-strike period. Attacks against the British Army and RUC were at an all-time high. Black told the RUC everything he knew. Actually, he knew very little. He was able to relate only one instance of an actual killing, one wounding and eleven cases of false imprisonment. The false imprisonments involved the Provos taking over local houses as a base from which to launch operations. Black disappeared into protective police custody, and his wife and children were spirited away by the RUC. The RUC said there were only four Provos left in North Belfast after Black was finished. Black told the RUC that most of those they wanted could be got more easily around nine each night, when they visited their families. He gave away the location of a Provo training camp off the Donegal coast. Eleven armalite rifles and 4,000 rounds of ammunition were recovered following a raid. Black himself was hidden in England and didn't appear for a preliminary enquiry. The Director of Public Prosecutions activated the Voluntary Bill of Indictment process to bypass the process whereby Black would have to give evidence twice. With relatives of the accused in court that would entail emotional pressure for Black. He might, for example, decide to retract under those circumstances.

In 1982 Black made further statements to the police. There were differences between his first and second set of statements. The judge said that those differences could be explained by the fact that Black was a very frightened man when he first talked to the police. The trial started at the end of 1982 and was to last 117 court days. It was the first informer case of such major importance to reach the courts in the North. Black faced the single judge for the time he was giving evidence. He refused to look at those he accused. Each defendant was allowed one relative in court, and the proceedings went ahead at a leisurely pace, as the judge wrote down everything in longhand. Maps of alleged incidents were spread on a dais in front of him. Dozens of RUC men and women wore their bottle green uniforms, the warders were in blue and Lord Justice Kelly wore scarlet robes. All this was in striking contrast to the defendants, pale and poorly dressed by comparison. Black had two 'minders' throughout the trial. Lord Justice Kelly thought Black a very impressive witness and complimented him on his memory. Black had recounted to the court, among other things, how he had committed perjury in 1975 to give himself a false alibi on the robbery charge. He recounted his own part in how he tried to kill people. Thirty-five people went down on his word alone and got more than 4,000 years in jail between them. In the two years between the date Black was first arrested and when he gave evidence, twenty-eight more informers had decided to give evidence. Most followed the same pattern as Black. People were arrested from their homes, denied bail and spent years in jail waiting for the trial to come up. Many were given immunity, new identities, money to settle abroad. 200 people were awaiting trial on their word alone. If their cases were followed on a pro rata basis, those 200 people were due around 62,000 years between them. Most were charged on the word of the informers alone, and in some cases, there wasn't even evidence that incidents ever took place, as with conspiracy charges, for example.

The effect on the nationalist community of informers was devastating. There were also loyalist informers. They tore communities apart. People started to look at one another again. With typical Belfast humour, the graffiti started to appear—'I knew Christopher Black but thanks be to fuck he didn't know me.' Most informers had been in the thick of it for years. Most could see no end in sight, and could not see what progress, if any, their own organisations were making. Most had been in jail, and when they were arrested may have incriminated themselves. Many were offered immunity and a new life at this point.

In August 1983, as the final preparations were being made to leave the prison in the food lorry, William Skelly was arrested. He named twenty-nine men in the Beechmount and Ballymurphy areas of Belfast. He named one man as being involved in a rocket attack and a kidnapping. That man was Robert Lean. The RUC arrested them all. Skelly was brought face-to-face with Lean in Castlereagh. Skelly also mentioned Lean's wife and there was a possibility that she would also be charged. She was the mother of five children. Lean started to talk. He signed numerous statements. The police said that Lean was a big fish, he was portrayed as a master spy. He was number two in Belfast. He named people who were supposed to be at the top. He named Gerry Adams but refused to meet him face-to-face in Castlereagh, saying that Adams was very popular and he didn't want to put undue pressure on his own family. He did confront

70

other people. Lean's wife was taken into protective custody. Lean was told that he would be resettled in a country of his choice and pensioned off. He was guarded by 'minders' and moved from one British Army base to another. He was a 'free agent' and a 'converted terrorist' the police said. They also said that the Belfast OC and Chief of Staff were going to be nailed. There was panic.

Dozens of people were arrested. There was the possibility that some of them might crack and give the escape away. The Belfast Brigade was supposed to supply some of the back-up for the escape. There were ructions within the prison. The plans had been laid for the best part of a year and now an informer was spilling the beans. The question was, how much did he know. People went on the run. There were leaks in the media in which informed police sources were quoted as saying that there would be further arrests. Road blocks were increased throughout the North. The impression was created that the police were looking for people to arrest. Fifteen days before the escape, seven were arrested in Belfast. This was followed two days later by nine more. The word went out that Lean was going to put everyone away. The reason he was going to put everyone away was that he was high up in the movement. The logic went that those named must be guilty if he was so high up. Belfast Brigade was told to take a hike for the duration of the escape.

Papillon and the second man from the Escape Committee talked about Lean in the metal fab shop that day. Lean wasn't a problem, Lean knew nothing. The escape would go ahead. But there was now a gap in the escape which would have to be filled by other brigades, most notably Armagh. But even if Lean knew nothing there was still a problem because some of those arrested on Lean's word might know something, and some of them might talk. There was just no way of knowing.

Part of the confidence in the back-up was due to the fact that Brendan Burns and Brendan Moley would be taking part. Burns came from a strong republican background and had joined the IRA full time in 1976. He was a competent and thorough operator and well known to the security forces. Moley was one of a family of nine children, had been a joiner but had gone on to full-time active service with the IRA. Both operated out of Armagh and knew the county extremely well. Both knew what would be required to bring the escapees to safety.

There were other problems as well. A crucial comm had gone missing. It contained the latest list of people going on the escape, the final instructions for the outside, routes, dates. The comm was sufficiently coded that it wouldn't give everything away. If the prison authorities got their hands on it, they would know that there was something going down. The warders had started a work-to-rule and this meant that movement between the Blocks was upset. Communication was difficult, it necessitated sending comms by circuitous routes. Where was the missing comm? Even when the work-to-rule was finished, the workshops weren't reopened immediately. So comms were sent out when the men went on visits, passed from one woman to another, and then sent back in to where they were required. The comm that had gone missing was intended for Papillon. It had gone out on a visit all right, but the man who was supposed to take it back in missed his visit. It was passed on to somebody else. Eventually it turned up safe. After two days.

7

Countdown

There was free association throughout H7 in the last few weeks before the date set for the escape. The men could move from one Wing to another for a chat with their friends. The movement had to be stopped. The Provos were using that movement and access to get messages to people taking part in the planning of the escape, and they didn't want the route of communication jeopardised for the sake of someone having a talk with a friend. Again, some people objected to this order. It appeared that no valid reason was being put forward for the change in policy. The plan was still a well-kept secret in those last couple of weeks. There were two people in H2 who knew about it, and no more than three in H3, though a good few people in H7 knew.

At the start of September, a prisoner was approached in the canteen of H7 by a senior IRA man. He was asked what he thought about escapes in general. Had he ever thought about escaping? He thought of little else, and he thought escapes were a good idea. He was asked to think some more on escapes.

A week later another IRA man came up to him. 'Have you thought anything more about escapes?' he was asked. He replied that if there was an escape happening, he would help out in whatever way he could. No, that's not what was meant. Would he go on an escape if there was one planned? He would. He was then told that there was one planned, that it involved taking over the Block and that there were a good few people going on it. Was he interested? He was. He was told not to mention it to anyone. He would be allocated a role on the morning of the escape. Even his own cell mate didn't know he was taking part.

Most people who were picked to go on the escape weren't told until the last possible moment. Their knowledge of the escape was limited to the part they themselves had to play. In those early days in September it must have seemed that prisons and prison issues were no longer rallying points for nationalists. Things were running smoothly in the Blocks. Secretary of State for Northern Ireland, James Prior, was talking about 'rolling devolution'. The prisons were quiet. Everybody was happy.

A week before the date there were still six men who were protesting and who refused to end it. They were all serving long sentences and saw the protests as the only way of expressing themselves effectively. It was a big step for them to end the protests. Gerry McDonnell agreed to end it; he was needed on the outside. Another man had a major part to play in the rear-guard action but refused to co-operate.

There were another two lifers on protest. One of them was John Pickering. But as soon as the two men ended their protest they were ordered to a committal Wing in H6 prior to their being allocated a working Block. This was unusual. The Escape Committee now faced a dilemma in the week of the escape. The two were lifers and would be good assets on the outside. They were advised not to go to the committal block if they were sent. They were to go back on the no-work protest. They were charged with refusing to work and ended up in the punishment Blocks. They were charged the Wednesday before the escape and would be due back in H7 on the day of the actual escape itself. The prison van would go out at around 2 pm and bring them back around 2.30 pm. This presented a problem.

In order for the Block to be secured well, it would have to be taken at the earliest possible time the food lorry was likely to arrive, and held until it actually did arrive. A prison van, plus an escort, could be pulling in to the front of H7 at the same time as the Provos were taking it over. Attempts were made to get a message to the two men that they were not to come back. There was some panic in H7 when it was realised that the two men were lost to the escape. In any event, the prison authorities never sent that van down for them that Sunday, and their lifeline was snatched away.

Searches were a problem in that last week. There were weapons moving around and they didn't want those found. The men had some idea when searches were due. They had orderlies everywhere. This gave the Provos an insight into how the warders were thinking, and when searches were coming down.

When the men were warned about a search the weapons and ammunition were moved to another area.

On the Wednesday before the escape a weapon was being carried from one Wing to another in H7 by a Provo. Suddenly, the Number One Governor appeared. At the same time there was a row going on between a prisoner and a warder over the fact that the warder refused to turn on the television. The man carrying the weapon shouted at the prisoner to stop arguing. The prisoner who was causing all the fuss knew that a weapon was being moved at the time. The Governor ordered the prisoner to be taken to the Boards and the weapon was moved safely.

C Wing was searched a short while before the escape but the weapons had been moved beforehand. At this stage H7 only had two of the five weapons they needed. A few nights before the escape the Quartermaster opened the dumps. They had the three remaining weapons which were passed on. It was at that point that the warders went on a work-to-rule and the RUC came in and took over their duties. So Papillon was stuck with a problem. They couldn't be moved through the workshops because there were none going on for so long as the work-to-rule continued.

All jail movement stopped and prisoners could only go out to the toilet. Papillon started to despair on the Tuesday night. Word was sent from H7 that they were going that Sunday with or without the weapons. Papillon decided to take a risk. The escape OC in H7 got a comm. All it said was, 'Enjoy your dinner.' Papillon paced his cell for the following few hours, nerves shattered. If the three weapons were caught, it would start a round of major searches and perhaps the escape would have to be cancelled. And yet without those weapons, there was little hope of taking control of the Block. As the hours passed, no alarm bells went off. No news was good news. A prisoner came over to Papillon later on that evening to say that the guns had reached H7. While not taking part in the action, and not having any control over what happened, he had managed to give H7 what it wanted. On that Saturday, there was an Irish class held in Cell 26 on one of the Wings in H7. Seven people were called into it. Kieran Fleming from Derry and Padraig McKearney were both there. They were briefed as to what part each had to play the following day. 'Are ye all on it?' asked the OC. They were all on it. He then gave a description of what was supposed to happen. The first stage people would take the Block. It was tricky in that it involved taking all the warders at the same moment. The second stage people would then have to secure the Block. This would mean making sure that telephones were not left unanswered and ensuring disciplined movement throughout the Block. The third and final stage was the rearguard. They would have to hold the Block while the thirty-eight men drove out in the lorry. They would have to give them enough time and then lock themselves back in their cells. It had to be timed so that they gave the lorry enough time to get away, and not long enough so that they would be caught out of the cells by the warders coming into the Block.

In each Wing trusted people were approached to take part in the rearguard. There was no shortage of volunteers for the job. There were five people on each Wing, two at the bottom, two at the top and one in the middle. A further two would stay at the panic button when the lorry started to roll. That brought the numbers involved in the last phase alone to almost thirty men.

All the IRA men were to wear ponchos and different shoes from those they normally wore. That way they would not be recognised. Nobody was to use actual names while the operation was going on. Everybody was to wear hoods and if possible there was to be no talk at all so that people could not be recognised by their voices. The impression would thus be given to the warders that they were dealing with crazy people, despite the nice behaviour they had witnessed over the previous few months.

Six people in each Wing would maintain control, and there would be a further four in each of the classrooms. There would be two more in the Circle, two in the prison officers' room and two in the Control Room. That was thirty-eight—the same number as were going out in the lorry. The night before the escape, the weapons were distributed and hidden in pillars throughout H7. Everybody was told of the implications of the operation if it went wrong. The rearguard were very important. They had to give the lorry enough time to get out. All potential evidence was to be set alight. They were also under orders to cause as much confusion as possible to delay the identification of the escapees. The cards on the cell doors were to be taken out and destroyed. When they returned to their cells, the men would to able to lock their doors from the inside using a rocking motion.

All those who by now knew about the escape were told that there would be a major back-up on the outside if everything went well. Not everybody knew where the link-up was to be made. Some were worried that the back-up might not be there. They were assured that it would be, that they would be able to telephone the Northern Ireland Office from Dublin to inform the authorities that they had escaped—if all went well. They might not literally be able to do this, but the back-up would be there. There would be a fifty-strong back-up unit, heavily armed, within ten miles or so of the prison. They would carry machine-guns and extra weapons for some of the escapees. The more experienced such as Seamus McElwaine and Padraig McKearney would be armed. A combination of the lorry and warders' cars would be used to reach the active service unit. The people using the cars would be the last to leave the prison; they would hold the last gate until the lorry was well clear, then they would follow it. Units from South Down, South Armagh and Tyrone would be waiting and the entire unit of about ninety would then move back into South Armagh. Other active service units would be sitting on landmines watching their backs as they moved deeper and deeper into the country. There would be communication using walkie-talkies. The escape would be a morale booster, a propaganda exercise and the IRA's biggest operation in its history.

A lot of people were worried about this back-up. And people were also worried about who was going, and who wasn't going. The men were told that some had been asked and had refused to go. Again and again, each went over the role they had to play, each memorised their part. There were men to take the warders and tie them up. Uniforms taken off the warders would be put into bags. The name of the warder would be written on the side of the bag. Nothing was to be taken from the warders apart from the uniforms. Some of the men would put on the uniforms to facilitate the taking of the last gate on the way out.

The signal to move was when the bumper was called for. Two men would be in the grilles, controlling movement into the four Wings. Everybody would move together. And a brief was issued. A brief was an IRA order. The word went down that if anybody interfered with the escape, they were to be dealt with. There were a lot of Provos in H7 who had no idea of what was planned. If a panic situation developed, such as a fist fight with a warder, it could blow the entire plan. People who were shadowing the warders were themselves shadowed—just to make sure everything went well. The men were ready to go.

8

Takeover and Breakout

On that Sunday morning there were 883 prisoners in Long Kesh. Fifteen of the twenty-eight occupied Wings contained republicans, six contained loyalists and seven were mixed. In H-Block 7 there were 125 men. Forty-four had been convicted of murder or conspiracy to murder, forty-one of possession or use of explosives; twenty-eight were in for possession or use of firearms; twenty-four were serving life; eighty-eight were serving sentences of ten years or more. Ninety-eight of the men were in their twenties and only seven were over thirty-five. Of the thirty-eight men due to go out in the lorry that day, twenty-eight had been convicted of murder or a similar offence. Five were in for explosive offences and five for firearms offences.

Sunday was a dull overcast day and time seemed to drag through the morning and early afternoon. There was a dry run of the escape before breakfast, just to make sure that the timing was right; it was. There were further briefings. People were nervous. Nobody wanted to be the one to ruin the escape for everyone else.

The Block was on a high. Men went around trying to act normally. Everybody knew that there was something happening. Some felt that the workshops were going to be smashed. Two of the escapees had no idea they were going on the escape until just before dinner time. But there were still problems. The guns had been worked on through the small hours of the night. One of the weapons had to be fitted with a silencer. There was no way of testing the weapon to make sure the silencer was working. Another weapon was giving trouble with the firing mechanism. It was fixed by using a part from a pen. Then all the weapons had to be cleaned down so that there were no prints on them. When the doors were opened that morning, all the five weapons and the one replica were moved into position. The people who were going to use them had to have easy access.

There was exercise as usual around ten that morning. The men couldn't believe that the day had actually come around. One man asked a friend in the exercise yard for the loan of his running shoes, in case he would have to run. He was told that if he had to run, the escape would be finished and that the shoes wouldn't be very useful. He didn't need running shoes. The plan was to drive away.

At Mass, people were given their final briefing. Most people that were going out turned up in their best clothes. Men who hadn't been to Mass in years suddenly appeared to be catching a dose of religiosity. There was a much bigger crowd than usual for Holy Communion. Small clusters of men could be seen hugging one another as they left Mass. There was a buzz going around. What made it worse was that everybody was trying to act normally and this was adding to the atmosphere. Some thought that the prison authorities had to notice something. While Mass was going on a final briefing was taking place in Cell 26 on the Wing in H7.

The weapons were handed out to the people who needed them. The roles people had to play were re-enacted again and again. The five leaders of the escape were fairly apprehensive, but they weren't really frightened. For three of them, it would be their only shot at getting out before the next century. Everyone was hopeful that they could get away. They also knew that the men staying behind were in a vulnerable position if warders decided to take their anger out on them. Repeatedly, people asked about the back-up and they were assured that it would be there. The rearguard went over the role again. Everybody understood what was involved if anything went wrong. Mass ended at about 11.30 am that day. The men went back to their own Wings. Then dinner followed and they were locked up at around 12.30 pm. That lock-up lasted until 2 pm, and it was during this time that the final preparations were made. The men were in their cells making masks. Some men took a haircut, others shaved off their moustaches, to give an added disguise. Some people gave mementoes to their cell mates, if they had any mementoes at all, while others were giving away shampoo and soap and other personal items. Some asked that personal belongings be sent to their families afterwards—if the cells weren't smashed up. Handicrafts were given away. There were three orderlies in the canteen during that lock-up, who had ensured that all windows in H-Block 7 were closed. If there was screaming and shouting they didn't want the noise to travel to the nearby British Army Observation Posts. The record player in each Wing was blaring at full volume; radios were on. It was around 2 pm when the warders came back from their own meal and unlocked the men.

The 125 prisoners appeared to be going about the normal Sunday routine, moving freely from Wing to Wing. Twenty-four men were employed as orderlies. There were twenty-four staff on duty, sixteen supervising the four Wings and six at various posts controlling movements. The Medical Officer was in his room. Tea would be served throughout the Block around 4 pm.

The warders let the men out and the workshops were opened. Immediately, anything that was going to be used as a weapon was secured. One man made sure the prisoners didn't complain about planes, chisels and hammers going missing. The weapons were taken out and allocated to people who would need them. Anybody who was allocated a role to take a warder would be armed with something. All warders and alarm buttons were being watched. Padraig McKearney had been ironing his jeans and t-shirt all morning. He rubbed the iron back and forth, back and forth. Nobody seemed to notice him at all. He was positioned between a warder sitting in a chair and an alarm button. When the word came to move, McKearney's idea was to use the iron to stop the warder making any moves towards the alarm button. There was another man backing up McKearney if anything went wrong. It was the exact same throughout the Block. Kieran Fleming was bouncing a ball and casually watching his warder. Fleming would give the word to his Wing. Everybody would move together. McKearney's warder went off to the toilet. There was to be no maltreatment. All warders would be taken to Cell 26, stripped, and then tied to each other in the classrooms.

Brendan Mead had given each of the other four some gum to chew to calm their nerves. Mead noticed that McFarlane was wearing his brown overalls. McFarlane always liked to look spic and span.

81

Bobby Storey, McFarlane, Mead, Gerry Kelly and Tony McAllister were all moving around the Circle. Mead had slagged McAllister for blessing himself before the operation started. Each carried a gun. Gerry Kelly was pushing the bumper. When that bumper was called for, there would be a mental countdown of ninety seconds before everyone would move.

Mead was supposed to go into the office and keep the senior officers busy. He panicked when he saw George Smylie standing outside the office. Storey reassured him that he would be able to handle it. Mead was nervous. He would now have Smylie following him into the office and therefore have less control over him.

Mead started to talk about his personal problem with Smylie and Smylie let him into the office. Kelly saw that McGlinchey and Kerr were in place at either end of the Circle. Both were between their two gates. Kelly could see everything, see McFarlane moving into the Hall. The door was opened and McFarlane produced his gun. Now!

Mead was talking about the fact that some of the men were giving him a hard time and he didn't know whether to leave the Block or not. Acting Principal Officer Robert George was also in the office. Mead produced the gun and told both men to hit the deck. The gun looked very real but Smylie lashed out and struck Mead on the side of the face. Mead screamed 'I'll blow you away'. He was already on the ground. And then Storey walked in. Storey shouted at Smylie to stop but was pushed away. Then Mead put a gun to George's head and said that if Smylie didn't knock it off, he would kill him. Smylie stopped and was tied up on the floor. George was left in a chair beside him. The prisoners thought he was going to die he looked so bad. They treated him very carefully.

C Wing was fairly typical of what happened throughout the Block. Some of the men were hiding in a cell as they waited for the word to go. One man wore a donkey jacket, a mask, and carried another replica weapon. There was a buzz going around the Wing. Fifteen people knew what was happening—ten would-be-escapees and five of the rearguard. The ten minutes after two that afternoon seemed like an eternity. The men were moving into position beside warders and alarm bells. The five lifers got into the Circle. Everybody could see what the person below them was doing: the men in the Circle could see the men at the grilles, the men at the grilles could see the men watching the warders and alarms. 'Lean agaibh ar aigh' was all the man in C Wing heard. They then heard two thuds. It sounded like shots but they couldn't be sure. They took their Wing in less than ten seconds. In fact, the entire Block was taken at the same time.

John Adams was looking the other way when Kelly pulled the silver .25 from his pocket. He took a two handed stance with the weapon—he had practised it often. Kelly then lowered his frame behind the gun so that Adams would see nothing but the top of his head and the weapon two feet from his face when he turned around. Kelly hoped that Adams would notice the aggression also.

'Don't fucking move an inch or I'll blow your head off' shouted Kelly, 'don't touch anything at all. Do exactly as I tell you and you'll be all right. Put both hands on your head'.

Adams put both hands on his head and he was told to kneel on the floor. John Adams went down and Kelly used one of his hands to open the grille. He told Adams that if an alarm went off he was to say it was an accident and re-set it.

Adams was lying right up against the door and Kelly had the gun pointed straight at his head when Kelly saw the toilet door open. A prison officer walked out. Kelly swung the gun around and ordered him onto the floor. The officer staggered back as if to make an attempt to get back into the toilet. There were windows in there. He could shout and warn people. He could give the game away. Kelly's mind was travelling at a million miles an hour. Kelly was turning back towards Adams when he noticed the door of the Control Room being slammed shut. Kelly shoved his shoulder to the door. It moved. But Kelly couldn't leave the door because then John Adams would have an opportunity to press one of the alarms in the Control. The door could only be opened from the inside. There was an intercom to the Emergency Control Room, telephones, alarm buttons and a radio set. Kelly managed to get his arm around the door which was partially open. He fired two shots. On the second shot, he felt Adams slump against the door. He continued to point the weapon at Adams and he appeared to be dead. 'Are you okay John?' asked Kelly.

'I think so' he replied.

'Where were you hit?'

'I think I'm hit in the eye'.

John Adams had been hit just above the left eye. And there was panic among the men as they realised that a warder had been shot. Medical attention was looked for. The sound of the shots had gone all over the Block. The men didn't know if they had gone outside the Block.

McFarlane had been at the door leading into the Hall. He was carrying a mop and asked to be let in to clean it up. James Gwilt let him in. Gwilt heard the shots and looked around. He felt something hard being pressed against his side. He saw McFarlane with the gun and lay on the ground right away. The area was secured and McFarlane moved on.

McAllister and Storey were in the Circle. Osmond Murphy, another warder, was called over to the Officers Mess by McAllister. As Murphy walked into the Mess he was confronted by a prisoner with a gun. It was a small gun with a silver-coloured barrel. Murphy's only comment to the man with the gun was 'You're joking'. He wasn't. Storey was also armed. A few seconds before Murphy had reached the Mess McAllister and Storey had produced their weapons to the four prison officers drinking tea and said 'This is it, lads'.

One of the warders was asked about his car, its colour, make, registration, where it was parked. He was asked about alarms and security. He was asked these same questions by several people, just to make sure that he wasn't making it up. Other warders were also asked about their cars and where they were.

Prison Officer Kevin Palmer was between the grille controlling movement between A and B Wings. He never knew who put the screwdriver to his throat. There were four other warders in A and B. All were brought to cell 26, stripped, clothed in ponchos, hooded, and brought to the classrooms. They were then tied together. At one point, a hooded prisoner said, 'Don't leave them naked. Don't humiliate them like they humiliated us when we were on the blanket'.

Between C and D Wings, Prison Officer William McVeigh was on duty. Robert Kerr was bringing empty food containers through when the word came to go. Kerr produced a gun and McVeigh was grounded and both doors to the Wings were opened.

Prison Officer Walter Graham was near the dining-room

when he felt the pain in his left shoulder. He had been stabbed. He saw Kelly holding a gun at the Control Room. He went down immediately. Prison Officer Raymond Doherty was in the women's toilet, the men's being already in use. He knew there was something wrong when he heard the noise. He stayed behind the door for a while, wondering what to do. He came out eventually, and was grounded and tied up.

There was panic as soon as it was realised that a warder had been shot. Some of the men, dressed in ponchos and masks, began to address each other using their real names. They were ordered to stop using names. The only term to be used was 'Volunteer'. A prisoner raced to the Medical Room but the door was locked and there didn't seem to be anybody about. The job of the Medical Officer was to make up prescriptions and carry out various treatments as ordered by doctors. Ten minutes after the takeover, Medical Officer Stanley Nevins stepped out of the Medical Room and walked into the Circle. The Provos in the Circle were horrified—he had been left alone. Gerry Kelly, standing there in the Circle couldn't believe his eyes. Nevins had a telephone in the office, he might have used it. There was no way to knowing if he had made a call. The silencer hadn't worked on the gun and everybody had heard the shots. Kelly held the gun now, and with both hands extended, ordered Nevins on to the ground. He was then taken to the tea-room. John Adams was still conscious and was taken to the toilets. Nevins was moved again to treat him. The Provos now had control of H7 and they had a list of priorities. They wanted a controlled, disciplined approach to the escape. They wanted to stamp an air of authority on it and everybody was ordered to co-operate with Nevins in whatever he wanted. Six prison officers had been injured in the takeover, most of the injuries occurring because the prisoners were tense and nervous. All radios and televisions and record players were still turned up fully. All prisoners were told to go to their cells, but not to lock the doors. Then someone shouted to close the main door. It had been open throughout and it was possible that the takeover had been seen. Again, there was no way of knowing for sure.

The warders were brought to Cell 26, their uniforms taken and they were clothed in panchos and hoods. They were taken to the classrooms and tied to each other. The hoods were lifted every now and then and their faces were fanned with a table tennis bat. The uniforms were brought to the Circle by the prisoners who controlled the movement between the Wings. Those who were going to take the Tally Lodge on the way out started to dress up as warders. Another warder was brought to the Control Room to answer any telephone calls. The Provos in the Circle were running the show and the orders were issued from there.

The prison officers were shocked and bewildered. They could scarcely believe what was happening, and didn't know what was going on. The prisoners felt great. Some of them had been in jail for ten years and felt great at having a measure of control over their own lives. But the plan had been spoiled by the shooting of John Adams.

The Provos took photographs of the operation. They photographed all their files in the Block. Then they burned them in order to confuse the prison authorities. Intelligence reports on prisoners were photographed and burned. Names and cards on the doors were changed or destroyed. The files were all checked to find out what the prison authorities knew about each and every prisoner. Warders were asked their height when their uniforms were taken. This was written down on each bag used to carry the uniforms. The prisoners could pick a size that suited them.

Then a statement was read out to all IRA and INLA prisoners, to the effect that the IRA had taken control of the Block, that there was an escape on, but that not everybody was going on it. Prisoners were ordered to go to their cells. The statement also said that anybody who wanted to go on the escape, could go. But the prisoners didn't have any real choice. The statement would cover them afterwards. They would be able to claim that they had stayed behind voluntarily. The Provos said that any prison officers who were involved in ill-treatment afterwards would have their names forwarded to the outside, where they would be dealt with. There was just the waiting for the lorry. The lorry was late.

Before the lorry came, a paper van called to H7. The papers were thrown out to a prisoner wearing a prison officer's uniform at the gate. Meanwhile, the escapees were shown a map of where they were going. They had to memorise the map and then it was destroyed. The lorry was twenty minutes late. The prisoners' feelings were veering between euphoria and depression.

The lorry drove into the yard and turned. It reversed to allow the food to be unloaded. The prisoners were very tense. If they made one wrong move, the entire plan would fall through now. David McLaughlin was driving the lorry and Dessie Armstrong was the kitchen orderly helping him. As the lorry stopped McLaughlin was confronted by Bobby Storey, waving a gun at him. McLaughlin was taken from the lorry, shown the guns and the ammunition, shown John Adams and the other six warders. He had little choice but to do what he was told. A string was tied under the driver's seat in the lorry, connected to a grenade, he was told. If he didn't co-operate, the pin would be pulled by Gerry Kelly, who would be lying on the floor of the lorry. Kelly would also have a gun trained on him.

The tea was a salad that day, and it had to be unloaded by the men in the Circle. The order went out to the Wings to 'sit tight' and that they would be 'given the word' when the time was right. That wait was an eternity. There was a call to H7 from another Block. Had the food lorry left H7 yet? Was it going to be long? It wasn't going to be too long, just a while more. A prison officer was being forced to answer the phone. Three prisoners went looking for tobacco to roll a cigarette. They arrived in the canteen and found some. Suddenly, they were told to 'move out'. They grabbed their coats from their cells and shook hands and hugged those they were leaving behind. One man was left with the keys of the cells on each of the four Wings. Anybody not going would be locked in and the rearguard would lock themselves in after that.

'Those with no prison officers' uniforms get into the back of the van'. About twenty-five men started to clamber aboard. Robert George looked at his watch. It was just 3.55 pm.

Padraig McKearney went around to nearly everybody. One man, who had lost his leg in an explosion was almost crying. He really wanted to go. There were emotional scenes as the men said goodbye to each other. One man carried a bag of clothes to the lorry. He was asked if he was going to Bundoran on his holidays. 'Yeah I am', he answered. He was ordered to leave the bag behind, there was simply no room in the lorry. He turned back into B Wing. He was the last man there. As he walked back to the lorry, he shouted into the silence down the Wing, 'Tiocaidh ar la.' The sound of his voice echoed up and down the Wing and back through the Block. By now the Provos had had control of the Block for an hour and a half. The rearguard started to gather stuff together in the Circle so that it could be burned. They would hold the Block for as long as they could. A silence had enveloped the Block. The prison officers noticed that things went quiet for a short while. The rearguard kicked up noise to give the impression that everybody was still there.

In the back of the lorry everything was explained again. The number of gates they would have to go through, and what was likely to happen. They were told about the Tally Lodge. At the Tally Lodge the men with the uniforms would take it over and stay behind to let the lorry get away. They would follow later in warders' cars. They were also told that if any warder at any of the gates found out what has happening, they would have to take him prisoner and replace him with somebody in uniform. People were picked at that point to replace any warders they had to take.

Each man that was to be armed was now informed of the fact. Seamus McElwaine talked with another escaper about the finer points of using a Garrand rifle. He had never used one before and wondered if they were difficult to operate. Padraig McKearney and Kieran Fleming were also to be armed. The criterion for handing out weapons was the length of time people had spent in jail: those who had been in the shortest time were chosen. But there was a problem giving Kieran Fleming a weapon. He had a broken arm. He had been messing about in the yard when it happened and had gone to the doctor. He didn't want to be taken to hospital and had cringed with pain as the doctor had tested his arm by bending his fingers. He had assured the doctor that his arm was fine. It wasn't; it was broken. He had told very few people about his injury, knowing that he would be knocked off the escape if he admitted it. Now his weapon was assigned to someone else.

The shutters were rolled down on the back of the lorry. Everybody was under orders not to talk. It was very dark, but each man could just make out the outline of the face of the man next to him. It was hot, too. The men were sweating with tension and fear. Crouched in a small area, the men listened as the driver was brought out. He had been told repeatedly what he was expected to do.

By the time David McLaughlin was brought to the lorry, the shutters were already down. The men in the Circle had used the escalator on the lorry to take the trays of food out. He wasn't sure exactly how many were in the load in the back. He got into the lorry, and his foot was tied to the clutch. He was told that the lock on the driver's side was broken and that it would be pointless to try and get out. There was also the 'grenade' under his seat. The string was tied to the pin. Gerry Kelly crouched on the floor. Armstrong was riding beside McLaughlin in the passenger seat. The Happy Wagon moved away from H-Block 7.

The men in the back of the lorry could see very little outside. There were small holes in the bottom of the lorry but they had blocked these off with coats in case warders should take a look through them. They could see condensation building up on the inside from all the heat and tension. Back in the Block the rearguard were gathering everything in the Circle. People were told to stay quiet and to keep their radios on in their cells. Gradually, the rearguard retreated until there was just one man left in uniform. He kept an eye on the warders locked up in the classrooms, the medical officer, and the two senior officers in their office.

The first gate the lorry came to was the Segment Gate. People were talking and whispering. Storey ordered them to shut up. Most of the men were hunkered down, their legs going numb from holding the same position. The prison officer was whistling at the Segment Gate. The men in the back of the lorry could hear him. They heard his footfalls move up the side of the lorry and then the gate was opened. They moved off again. They breathed a sigh of relief and headed towards the Administration Gate. Prison Officer Thomas Ireland was on the gate that day. He noticed nothing unusual about the lorry. The men in the back of the lorry heard the rattling of his keys. He hummed to himself as he opened the gate; it seemed to the men in the back of the lorry that they had been there for years. They had only been a few minutes.

As they moved off, someone asked 'Where are we now?' Each had a mental picture of where they were. They were heading now for the blind spot, the spot just before the next security gate. They pulled in and the shutters went up. The escapees who were dressed as warders now got out and wiped the sweat off their faces. Some of them were armed and they walked towards the Tally Lodge as calmly as they could. The Tally Lodge was where each and every person entering and leaving the prison was checked. They wanted to take the Lodge. They would leave some of their own men there after taking control. David McLaughlin watched from the lorry as the first prison officers at the Tally Lodge were taken prisoner. Dessie Armstrong was taken out of the passenger seat and left with the warders. Gerry Kelly now ordered McLaughlin to drive up as far as the main gate. McLaughlin continued to watch as more and more prison officers started to arrive at the Lodge. He moved his lorry forward.

One escaper had walked to the Lodge with a paper over his arm and a gun concealed underneath. He had been worried about being recognised. It was crucial to take the Lodge in order to get the lorry out. Bik McFarlane, dressed as a warder, moved down the side of the lorry at the same time. McLaughlin was supposed to drive out the gate as far as Blaris Road. He was then to be tied up and left in a field.

Back in H-Block 7 there was another voice on the intercom. The rearguard had retreated by now. They had used lighter fuel to burn papers and masks in the Circle. The remains were smouldering. The lorry should have left at 3.35 pm. But it had been late. By 4 pm it should have been ten miles from the prison. The men in H7 had no idea where the lorry was. They could only presume that it had cleared the prison.

One man in H7 noticed a bag with about sixty rounds of ammunition in it. He flung it down the Wing, away from his own cell door. When the intercom had crackled into life the first time, a prison officer had been forced to answer it. Now it was crackling again, and the prison officer was tied up. Again and again, a voice came across on the intercom 'Is that 7? Is that 7? Is there any problem?' There was no answer. The buzzers all over H7 started to ring and ring and ring. Nobody answered.

Prison Officer Baden Cordner had come back to work through the Tally Lodge. Prison Officer James Ferris gave him a short rub-down search and his pass was changed. Baden Cordner walked on through. He went through the Lodge and headed for the next gate. He noticed something very odd indeed. He saw men getting out of the back of the food lorry which was parked close to the gate. He recognised Bobby Storey right away. Storey breezed past carrying what looked like a gun. 'This is for real', he said, 'we haven't come this far to be stopped now. If you try to run or shout a warning you're dead.' He took Prison Officer Cordner into the Transport Office. Cordner was told to follow orders.

90

Prison Officer Samuel Scott was on the Inner Gate at the Tally Lodge. His job was to open the gates and let vehicles into the airlock, between two gates. A man came around from the passenger side of the food lorry, pulled a newspaper off his arm, and showed Scott the gun. He was brought into the search area of the Tally Lodge.

Prison Officer Wright had been in the same search area when a man with a gun had taken him prisoner. Gerry Kelly kept watch over the prison officers that had been taken. When the phone went in the Lodge, Wright was ordered to answer it. There was a prison officer, a colleague, on the far end. He was enquiring if another colleague was at work that day. Wright was very abrupt. 'No', he answered. He slammed the phone down. There was a call back from the same prison officer. Was everything all right at the Lodge? Wright told him that everything was fine. 'What do you think is wrong?' he asked. 'There is nothing wrong.' And he slammed the phone down again. His attempt at trying to tell his colleagues there was indeed something wrong had apparently failed. Prison Officer James Ferris was unco-operative. When he was confronted by a man carrying a gun he started to shout. He ran from the Lodge and he bumped into other prison officers on their way in. He shouted at one man to run. James Ferris was stabbed in the chest. All the prison officers were taken back inside. There were two British Army Observation Posts overlooking the scene. To the soldiers looking on, it looked as if there were warders fighting with each other. James Ferris was brought in and tied up. Then large numbers of prison officers started to come into the Tally Lodge. Many were returning from their break. There was also a shift change taking place. The significance of the lorry being twenty minutes late arriving at H7 now took on an added dimension. Officers coming into the Lodge were now confronted by escapees wearing uniforms and carrying guns. They were brought to the search area. The numbers started to add up. Eventually, there were more than forty prison officers all piled up on top of each other in the search area. Two Provos wearing uniforms and brandishing guns were trying to keep control of them. Prison Officer Samuel Matier was in the Tally Lodge. When he was confronted with a gun, he thought that it was a British Army exercise. A lot of prison officers thought the same. They couldn't believe what was happening. Matier had worked himself close to the alarm button gradually. He moved a little every time another officer was brought in. The red button was under the TV monitor. He managed to pull the alarm without being seen. The Emergency Control Room came on the intercom immediately. They wanted to know why the alarm was on if there was anything wrong. Prison Officer Wright was forced to answer them. There was nothing wrong. Control asked that the alarm be reset. Wright asked them how that was done. Control told him to pull it out and that the alarm would reset itself. As a senior officer, Wright knew very well how to reset the alarm. His attempts to tell Control that there might be something wrong in the Tally Lodge had also apparently failed. But things were getting very hot for the escapees. There were simply too many prison officers coming into the Lodge and they weren't able to control them all.

Prison Officers Edward Hudson and Reginald McBurney were coming back into the prison. They noticed that the pedestrian gate was closed. The vehicle gates were open. They saw a man in uniform coming towards them. McBurney recognised him at once. 'McFarlane you bastard, what are you doing here?' shouted McBurney. McFarlane didn't take the trouble to reply, and bolted back into the Tally Lodge. Hudson and McBurney also ran, blowing their whistles. McBurney shouted to Prison Officer William McKane, who was parked just outside the gate. McBurney shouted at him to drive his car in front of the gate, to block it off. McKane drove the car towards the gate and blocked off the exit. He then got out of the car, locked it and drew his baton. Inside the search area of the Tally Lodge, the prison officers that had been taken captive could hear the melee starting. One of them jumped on Bobby Storey and started to struggle with him. Another joined in. Storey lost his gun, and all of the prison officers started to get off the ground. To stall them, Storey shouted, 'Okay, you win, we lose.' It was a last-ditch attempt to maintain some discipline and to try and retrieve the situation. It restored order slightly, and gave people a chance to bolt for the gate.

Storey got to the back of the lorry and threw up the shutters. There was a long lonely wail as the alarm started to go off. Alarms were going off all over the prison by now. The men in the back of the lorry were sure that it was all over. Storey shouted into the lorry. 'Right boys, the ball's busted. Everybody out.' The escapees started to pour out of the back of the lorry. The prison officers got a fright. They hadn't known that there were so many. They thought they wre dealing with a few escapees in uniform.

There was one prison officer in the Control Box at the Tally Lodge. He controlled the lever for the hydraulic gate. There was a sealed welded box with a slit in it to accommodate the control key. If something went wrong, that key was to be withdrawn and deposited in the box. It could not be retrieved and so the gate couldn't be opened. Seamus McElwaine had a gun pointed at the prison officer. He told him to open the gate fast. The gate was about six inches open when the melee started. Then inside the caged box, where he couldn't be got at, the officer was trying to pull the key out and dump it. The men from the back of the lorry had by now reached the gate and were hauling like crazy on it. This was their only and last chance at freedom. Suddenly, the gate just burst open. Prison officers were all over the place, blowing whistles. There was screaming and shouting and the barking of dogs. The scene was one of sheer panic. Some warders were trying to get away. There were scenes of hand-to-hand fighting between prison officers and escapees. The escapees ran a gauntlet of prison officers as they made their way towards the wire. Some of them wondered why the prison officers weren't trying to do anything to stop them. Everybody headed towards the wire, spread low over the ground. At the car park, just outside the gate, there were escapees trying to get into prison officers' cars. As they all headed for the wire Gerry Kelly had to be helped. The escapees could hear the sound of shots being fired. Almost immediately, three of the escapees—Robert Kerr, Denis Cummings and Edward O'Connor—were caught near the Tally Lodge. They were taken as they tried to hold back the prison officers, to stop them getting to the majority of men running away.

As all hell broke loose in the Tally Lodge area, James Ferris was brought to the kitchen. Two other men who had also been stabbed were also brought in. James Ferris said he was sick, he didn't feel too good. He was placed on his side. He was moved onto his back when that didn't help. Then he just stopped breathing and there was no pulse. Attempts were made to revive him. But Prison Officer James Ferris was dead.

9

The Race for Freedom

People saw Harry Murray and Bik McFarlane run towards the gate. Both men appeared to be carrying guns. More than thirty men were trying to follow them. The original plan had been to drive out of the last gate, which was located beyond the Tally Lodge. That option was now gone forever and the men would have to try and make it through the wire on their own.

Prison Officer William Gallagher had driven his yellow Toyota Celica JIJ 4069 at the front gate to try and block the escapees. A colleague shouted at him to take his car out so that the gates could be closed. He started to reverse his car out of the gateway. Just then he saw a number of men coming out of the Tally Lodge, running very fast. Gallagher reversed the car, got out and then locked it. He threw away the keys.

Brendan Mead and Jim McCann saw the keys lying on the ground. Mead put his head down and raced like mad to get the keys before another warder also running for the same prize. Mead reached the keys a hairsbreadth before the warder, and bent down as if to pick them up. But then he suddenly came up and punched the warder on the chin and landed him yards away. Mead was extremely fit. Mead was drenched in sweat as the yellow car refused to start, he was breathing heavily from the running and fighting and now the car wouldn't start and there were people getting in from all directions.

A voice on the outside shouted to 'smash the windscreen'. Officer Hudson managed to get his baton to the glass of the car as it sped past him and away. It took the original route of the planned escape. Jazz McCann was at the wheel.

Prison Officers William McClure and Edward Montgomery were in the car park near the gates when the fracas started. McClure liked to eat his lunch in the car, read the papers and listen to the radio. When the fighting started, and McClure saw the yellow car take off, he started up his red Skoda and sped off after the escapees.

The yellow car passed some prison officers as it swerved along the road. One man, who knew the owner of the yellow car, thought it might have been involved in an accident earlier in the day, and paid very little attention to it as it drove past him at speed. In any event, the men in the car were wearing prison officers' uniforms.

Prison Officer Thomas Aiken was on the External Gate. He lifted the barrier to allow the wife of a prison officer into the airlock between the double gates. But before he could get the barrier down again, McClure had arrived in the red Skoda. The lights were flashing and his horn was sounding. McClure had passed the yellow car with the escapees. He shouted to make sure all the exits were sealed.

The telephones were starting to hum at that External Gate. Word went out that all movement was to be stopped. But it was already too late. Prison Officer Charles Talbot was just bolting the gate when he saw the yellow car come up behind the Skoda. He jumped clear just in time as the escapees rammed the gate. 'Jesus Christ' thought Jazz McCann. The yellow car was wedged in the gateway, and four men got out. They started to run. They exited via the passenger door, which was facing out of the prison. The driver got out of his door, which was facing into the prison, and was confronted by a number of prison officers. Talbot grabbed the driver but he pulled away and started to run. They were all running across the fields.

With his ears still ringing from the crash, Jazz McCann ran from the car. He was wearing a brown bomber jacket and brown trousers when Army Craftsman Philip Tipping shouted 'Army, stop or I fire'. McCann could not believe that he was about to be fired upon as he made his way along the road. A shot rang out but it wasn't anywhere near him. The second shot from the 9mm Browning whizzed past his head as he came to a corner in the road.

McCann went into what he thought was a newly ploughed field, and gradually began to slow down, trying to get his breath back. McCann saw the soldier come up close and saw the weapon waver in his hand. He stopped and silently cursed the prisoner who refused to lend him running shoes earlier on that day. As the soldier escorted him back to the prison, he passed a comment to a crowd of people on the side of the road. 'It was worth it' was all he said.

Prison Officer David Bole caught another man who staggered out of the car. He had been dazed by the crash. He was Jimmy Donnelly. McCann's only comment to the prison officers, after being caught—an attempt at some black humour in the circumstances—was, 'You're in trouble now, boys.' Both were strip searched. Nothing was found.

Meanwhile, back at the Tally Lodge, there was pandemonium. Harry Murray was out in the car park, waving a gun about. He was helping people across the wire. Billy Gorman was there. Gorman was overweight and was getting snarled up every time he tried to get across. Prison Officer John Courtney, who had been held prisoner at the Tally Lodge and who thought the takeover had been a British Army exercise, grabbed Gorman. Murray went back to help Gorman. A struggle developed between the three, with Courtney thinking the gun Murray had was a replica weapon. Courtney was shot in the thigh. Murray, thinking Gorman was away, ran across the wire. But Gorman was snarled up again and Murray went back to help him. That was when Prison Officer Billy McKane challenged Murray, who had a black gun with a silencer attached to it. Gorman was held and Murray took off, almost the last man away. McKane tried to fire after Murray but the gun appeared to jam. He freed the mechanism and fired a shot but he wasn't too sure if he hit anybody.

Gunner David Lee was with the Second Royal Field Artillery attached to the Guard Force at the prison. He had started that day at 2 pm and was positioned at Tower Golf, the high-level tower which overlooked the main gate, where the fracas developed. He noticed all the activity around 4 pm but thought there was nothing unusual. Then prison officers started to shout that there was an escape going on. He relayed the information across his Tannoy system and started to open his soldier's box, which contained a gun for firing baton rounds. He saw the large white Bedford food lorry in the airlock, and saw the men scrambling from it. He called the Operations Room. He needed help. He heard a shot when he was still trying to get his box open, so he loaded up his rifle and abandoned the box. He threw up the flap on the window which overlooked the car parks of the

Larry Marley (*Pacemaker*)

Paul Kane outside Dublin's Four Courts (*Derek Speirs/Report*)

Patrick McIntyre leaving the Four Courts (left) following his release from custody and making a hurried departure by motorbike (below) a few moments later (*Derek Speirs/Report*)

An aerial view of the Maze Prison (*Pacemaker*)

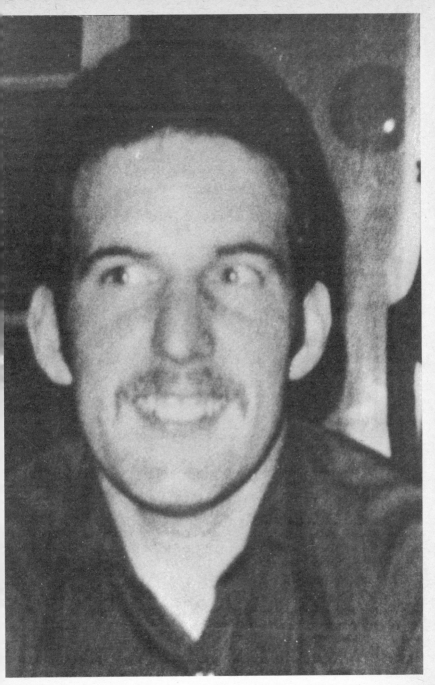

Bobby Storey (*Pacemaker*)

Robert Russell entering the Four Courts in Dublin (*Derek Speirs / Report*)

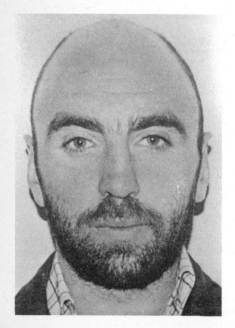

Gerry McDonnell (*Pacemaker*)

Gerry Kelly (*Pacemaker*)

Padraig McKearney (*Pacemaker*)

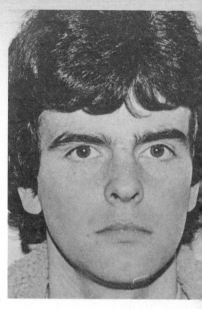

Seamus McElwaine (*Pacemaker*)

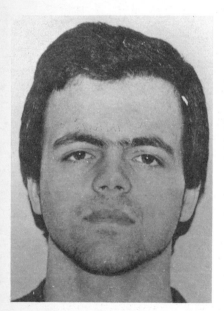

Kieran Fleming (*Pacemaker*)

Anthony McAllister (*Pacemaker*)

prison and where most of the prisoners were now located. He saw a prison officer lying outside the fence and a large number of men running up the field, escapees and prison officers. Some of the escapees were wearing prison officers' uniforms, some were in civilian clothing. Some of the prison officers were wearing their uniforms, but some of those who were just coming on duty were still in their civilian clothing. Gunner David Lee was confused as to what to do. Some prison officers were gathered around Officer Courtney, now lying on the ground outside the wire. 'He shot him, he shot him,' they roared, as they pointed up the field, away from the main bunch. 'Shot at who?' inquired Gunner Lee. The prison officers roared again. Gunner Lee shouted to Harry Murray, now about 100 yards away and disappearing fast: 'Halt or I fire!' Murray kept running, Lee fired, Murray spun around and fell to the ground. He had been shot in the leg.

Police Constable Colin Mulligan watched as the prison officers carried Murray back down. They left him a couple of feet from the perimeter wire. Mulligan thought he was dead, just lying there on the ground. He touched his head to see if he could get a reaction. Murray groaned and asked for medical attention. There was a three-inch hole in his thigh. Murray still had twenty-five years more of a sentence to serve. If he had not held back the warders at the wire, more would have been caught. But the RUC and UDR and British Army were putting plans to catch the men into action. As soon as the word went out that there had been an escape, vehicle checkpoints were put up automatically.

RUC Constables Colin McCord and Vincent Murphy were on Mobile Patrol in the Lisburn area, close to the prison, when they got the message across their radio about the escape. They set up a pre-destined roadblock near the prison at Eglantine Road. At 4.28 pm exactly, a green Volvo GIA 2974 approached. There were two men in the car. The man in the passenger seat was wearing a prison officer's uniform. McCord pointed his carbine at both men and ordered them from the car. Neither man moved. McCord then opened the passenger door and pulled the man in uniform from the car. The driver opened his door and got out. McCord ordered both men to place their hands over their heads. The man in the uniform had no identification. He said that he had someone else's jacket on, that he was going to see a relative in hospital. He said he lived in Twinbrook. McCord wasn't happy with his answers and arrested both men. As far as the passenger in the green Volvo was concerned, the game was up. He had run for five minutes after getting across the wire. He called at a house and asked the man who answered the door to take him to a hospital in Belfast. The man said that his wife was using the car but that there was a taximan living just across the road and he would take him. So the taximan took him in the green Volvo. The passenger's name was J. J. Burns. He had been burned out of Dover Street in Belfast in 1969 when the attacks on nationalists areas came. In 1972 he had joined the IRA the day after his nephew was shot dead. He had tried to escape on other occasions, and was in bad health with failing eyesight and a stomach disorder. He had served just seven and a half years of a thirty-year sentence.

Around the same time as Burns was getting picked up in the taxi, Constable Errol Reid was on Mobile Patrol near Dromore, also close to the prison. He was accompanied by two reserve constables. They got word to be on the lookout for a Southern-registered car which was believed to be involved in the escape. At exactly the same moment that Burns was stopped they set up a roadblock on a southbound carriageway, close to a viaduct. The two reserve constables were given the job of directing the traffic onto the hard shoulder on the road. And two minutes later, a blue Mercedes arrived. It was a bit slow pulling into the side of the road. Reid approached the fair-haired driver and asked him for identification. The driver appeared nervous and hadn't any identification with him. His passenger had a skin-head haircut, and was sweating. It wasn't that warm, and Reid was suspicious. The skinhead opened the door and got out. Reid asked the driver what his passenger's name was. 'McManus', came the reply. Reid went to the back of the Merc and asked the passenger his name. 'Kelly', he answered. Reid said nothing. He went back to the driver and asked him why his passenger had given a false name. And when asked for identification again, the driver just shook his head. He arrested both men and took them to Banbridge RUC station. Escapees Marcus Murray and Martin McManus were caught.

Back at the prison Dr Alistair Glasgow had arrived. In the kitchen in the Tally Lodge he examined James Ferris. He noted two puncture wounds to the right upper part of the abdomen.

The pupils of the eyes were dilated and fixed. The body was pulseless and the breathing was stopped. He pronounced James Ferris dead at 5.10 pm.

Anne Cadwallader worked for the BBC in the North. It had been a slow, boring Sunday afternoon when she got a phone call at home. There were rumours of a breakout from the jail. There might be nothing in it, she was told, but it was better to check it out. She jumped into her car and headed down the M1 motorway towards the prison. There were traffic jams all over the place. At one roundabout there were scores of police and British Army. She decided that there was some truth in the story. She took the car off the motorway and drove on the grass verge. She got stopped twice at security checkpoints, but the police didn't seem to be too sure of what they were doing. She was allowed through. Her British accent and British-registered car were her passport. She arrived at the main gates of the prison. Reporters were milling about the gate, clamouring for information. The RUC said the gates were closed off, there might be a bomb there. The reporters moved back. Cadwallader started talking to one RUC man. What was happening. 'Well,' he said, 'I shouldn't be telling you this. But about eight or nine men have got away.' Cadwallader thus had the word of a policeman that there had been an escape. She got to a local house where there was a telephone and went on the air.

Up near the River Lagan, the military police were easy to recognise with their distinctive red berets. There was a roadblock and the river was being searched. Cadwallader watched as police and British Army and prison officers moved along the river.

Senior Officer John Rodgers had been leaving the prison when he heard that there was trouble. He gathered three men at the main gate—McClenaghan, McKane and Hudson—and started to walk along the road. The four stopped a red Escort and asked the driver to give them a lift. They got into the car and met an RUC landrover with two men in it. The four prison officers got into the landrover and headed for the Moira road. But before they got there they ran into a roadblock. Constable Thomas Dillon and Reserve Constable Anthony Roy were on it. They had got a radio message to put Operation Vesper into effect. This was the code for an escape from the jail. They monitored their radio and were sure that escapees were heading their way in a van. There was confusion as to how the men were travelling. They decided, along with the four prison officers and the two RUC men, to search along the river. Reports were coming in that four men had been seen running through the fields.

Hudson and McClenaghan headed down one side and McKane and Rodgers took the other side. Dillon and Roy were also walking along the river bank. 200 yards into the field, they noticed the grass was trampled. They saw a storm drain, three feet in diameter, on the far side of the river and decided that it was big enough for men to climb through. They headed back to the bridge to check it out. When they reached the drain they noticed that weeds were shaking near the far bank where they had been a minute or so before. There was no wind. Dillon pulled his Walther pistol and shouted, 'Come out'.

A man emerged, twenty-five feet away. Roy had his gun pulled by now and he fired. The man in the water shouted, 'Don't shoot, I'm not armed.' Then another voice said, 'We're coming out and we're not armed.' There were four men in the river. The two policemen ordered them all to swim across, but one of them was unable to swim. Three escapees—Hamilton, Storey and Simpson—came across. They were strip searched on the river bank but nothing was found. McGlinchey was hauled out on the far side. Within minutes the four were on their way back to the prison. They had had a very short period of freedom, most of it spent breathing through reeds under the water.

The heavily-armed IRA unit was still waiting to meet up with the escapees. They stared to get anxious. They had no idea that things had gone badly wrong or that the escapees were now trying to get out of the area under their own steam. Not all of the escapees knew where the unit was waiting. The location had been disclosed on a need-to-know basis. But they were listening to the radio, and they started to hear the reports coming in. They decided that it was time to get out of the area. There was nothing they could do now. The escapees were on their own.

Back at the prison, Assistant Governor Alan McMullin had arrived. He had been at home around 4 pm when he got the call. He arrived less than an hour later and was given a rundown on what had happened. He went into H7 an hour later. There was absolute silence in the cells when the warders came running onto the wings. The doors weren't opened at once, as the warders waited until the RUC arrived. When the doors were finally opened, people were not all in their own cells. Sometimes there were three, four, five, and even six men in a cell. One particular Governor arrived into the Block carrying a shortarm. The place was in chaos. The remains of the fire was still smouldering. The prison authorities had no idea how many men were missing, or who was missing. They decided to do a head count, man by man. Their first count revealed that there were eighty-eight men in the Block—thirty-eight were gone. But they still didn't know who was gone.

Some prisoners were not in their own cells, and in any event, the name cards were gone from most of the doors. There was ammunition strewn around the Wing. A decision was taken to transfer all the men to H8. It was in the process of being painted and was vacant. They decided to identify each man as he was transferred. The prisoners' movement book was gone and they had to positively identify each prisoner. The prisoners were strip searched in the Circle of H7, handcuffed and taken to H8. The prisoners were very frightened. By now, they knew that a warder was dead.

The men in the Block said they were beaten and brutalised. The men were brought to a table in a Block, identified, and then made to run a gauntlet of dogs between H7 and H8. Some men said they were bitten by dogs. Sixty RUC men were used to transfer the prisoners. Six to ten dogs were also used. Up to forty men said they were beaten on that Sunday night. The prison authorities denied that the men were beaten or that they were bitten by dogs. The cells had been opened up first, and then frisk searches had been carried out. The cells were then locked up again and later the men were taken out one by one. A prison officer did attempt to get to the bottom of the allegations concerning the dog bites. Thirteen prisoners, according to medical opinion, might have been bitten by dogs. There was one 'definite', nine 'probable', two 'possible' and one 'doubtful'. It was noted in a subsequent report that the tunnel formed by the dog handlers were about fourteen feet wide. At some points the dogs were much closer to the prisoners. The person conducting the enquiry met a 'wall of silence'.

As night began to fall around the jail the entire area was securely cordoned off. Many of the reporters who had been there earlier had left to file copy for their newspapers. When some

101

tried to get back in later on they were refused access to the area. Anne Cadwallader continued to conduct interviews with local people who had had their cars hijacked. At the edge of the cordon she passed her tapes to a colleague. A hot water bottle and a toothbrush and some blank tapes were passed in to her. She stayed in the area, filing copy all night long.

She could hear shooting across the fields. Every now and then, another shot would go off. She listened to the RUC on their radios and found out when each of the escapees were caught. As the night wore on, the gap between the 'eight or nine' that was supposed to have got away, and those recaptured, narrowed. She walked around the prison, wearing a light beige macintosh. She had her hands over her head. Cadwallader wasn't taking any chances. While walking by a hedge, or a cabbage patch, it would suddenly start to move, and a British soldier would emerge with a weapon at the ready. The shooting gradually diminished. As far as the RUC and the British Army were concerned there were men on the loose and they were armed. The mood of the RUC was one of hysteria. Some of them were almost laughing. They couldn't believe what was happening, or that anybody could have escaped. They didn't look on the escape as any kind of security disaster. As the night got colder, Cadwallader got into her car and started to drive around and around the prison, monitoring what was happening. She was stopped the first few times, and then she was just waved on. She drove around all night. Later on, they found out about James Ferris and the mood changed.

James Hannah was a British soldier in 'B' Company of the Royal Highland Fusiliers based at Palace barracks in Hollywood in Belfast. Six soldiers had gone to the prison following the escape and they went out on patrol at 10 pm that night. They took up positions near the prison, behind a factory near the bridge where the roadblock had been earlier in the day, and where four of the escapees had been caught. Hannah was walking along the river when a man emerged from behind some trees and put his hands in the air. The man was on his own. He was escaper James Roberts. He was handed over to the prison authorities. But many of the thirty-eight men had managed to get away. They were split into two main groups made up of eight men in each by this time.

Seamus Campbell from County Tyrone had been the first

man across the barbed wire spread out along the ground. He could see himself passing over the wire with a giant leap, and could see a lace from his shoe catch the wire. He lashed out with his foot to free it. As he touched the ground, he looked back and could see dozens of others following on. And there were prison officers starting to run. Shots could be heard as the men scrambled up the field. One man noticed pieces of earth moving in front of him and then he could hear the sound of the shots afterwards. Meanwhile, Campbell was running up an incline and came to the top of the field. He knew there was a road up there somewhere. There was a bank on the far side and he slid down. Rabbits scurried out of his way on either side. The place looked like a disused sand quarry. He landed on his feet and started to run to a gate at the end of the field. He was joined by dozens of others. They could see a farmyard when they reached the road. Some children were driving an old banger backwards and forwards and they ran to the car. The children started to shout, 'Mister, mister, we've done nothing wrong.' They were frightened.

'Get out of that fucking car. Get out. We're the IRA and we need it.'

Eleven people managed to pile into the wreck. Padraig McKearney was there. There were bodies everywhere, including two who were hanging out of a window on either side. They started to move off very slowly. One man in the car shouted, 'There's screws after us.' A car was following them with warders. It managed to pass them out, and tried to stop the banger with the escapees. One escaper hanging out the window carried a shortarm. He tried to take aim and fire at the warder's car but the swerving of the banger put him off. The clutch started to go in the banger. There were simply too many people in it. And then, for whatever reason, the warders turned left and the banger went straight ahead. The escaper was still trying to take pot shots at them. They drove for about a mile and then four men decided that they would get another car. This was a red Ford. There was a young man sitting in the driver's seat, just testing the gears. A woman looked on from the front door of the house as one escaper ran to the car. He started to speak in Irish, and explained that they were the IRA and that they needed the car. All orders throughout the operation had been in Irish. The man behind the wheel didn't understand a word and the men still in the banger started to shout at him to speak in English.

Instead, he grabbed the man sitting behind the wheel and threw him over his shoulder. The woman at the door started to shout about her rights, that she knew people couldn't get away with this. The escapees weren't in any mood to listen.

Padraig McKearney took the wheel and four of them drove off. They were in great spirits. They had a good car and a chance to get away. Then they started to fight amongst themselves. One man wanted to head to Belfast and another wanted to get to the border. They just drove along with little idea of their eventual destination. They decided against going to Belfast because there would be house-to-house searches. They decided against the border because there would be roadblocks. They agreed to head for a small town which had a sympathetic nationalist population.

Cars were commandeered by various means. After the car with the bad clutch had to be dumped, four men were stranded on the road, three of them dressed in warders' uniforms. They saw a car coming along and one of them lay down on the road as if he were dead. Another escaper waved the car down. There was a woman driving and a man in the passenger seat. 'Help us, help us,' the escaper shouted, 'we've had an accident, can you take us to the hospital?' Two of them got into the car and then forced the man and the woman out. The 'dead' man on the road jumped up and a fourth appeared from behind a ditch. The car had a sunroof and there were two torsoes sticking out as they drove down the road. Again, they started to argue as to where they should go. Nobody knew where they were or where they were going. They just started to drive.

The four men in the red Ford taken from the house were giving each other the thumbs-up sign every few seconds. They hit the Moira roundabout doing almost 100 miles per hour.

Another car was commandeered from two old women who happened to be pulled into a lay-by. One of them was about eighty, the other fifty. Four escapees went over to the car. The younger of the two women was driving. The older woman started to get out when she were asked. 'Ah God, son' said the younger woman, 'my mother is sick, leave us alone.'

One escaper answered at once, 'Jesus, Missus, she's not half as sick as we are.' This group of four decided to follow McKearney. They had seen the car and knew what it looked like. They spotted the car up in front of the road and they pulled in right behind it and followed it to Dromore. It wasn't the right car; they were following the wrong car and knew they were lost. One of the men in the lost car saw a signpost for an area he recognised as being a nationalist area. They started to drive. They turned on the radio and the newsflashes were starting to come on. Already it was being dubbed the great escape. They listened to the football results. They got as far as Banbridge, and saw a signpost for Belfast. They were driving down through a small town, and then they saw something else which bothered them greatly. They were driving down the main street when they saw a warder from the prison out walking his dog. The men looked at the warder, and the warder looked at the men. They were sure that the game was up. They drove out of town, past the RUC station, all four of them thinking that they were going to be stopped at any moment. They drove in the direction of Castlewellan and decided that it was time to dump the car at the edge of a town. One of the escapers walked up to a young girl and demanded to know if she was a nationalist. The girl brought the men to her parents. Her mother said it was all right to stay in the house for a while. It was an hour or so before they made any contact with the local IRA, who went to get the car to dump it but there was a mix-up and the car was left in the area. They started to listen to the news, and learned of the prison officer who had died. They were sure that it was John Adams, the man who had been shot in the Circle at H7.

Meanwhile, another car had arrived at another town. It was pulling in at the side of the road when the escapees noticed two British Army jeeps coming their way. They ditched the car and walked into town. They stopped another young girl and asked her if she was a nationalist. Two men stayed in the car, two went with the girl.

McKearney hit the Moira roundabout at top speed. All the four men in the car could see was an armoured-plated RUC vehicle facing them, coming from the opposite direction. Its lights were flashing, its siren was going. The four in the car drove around the roundabout and then headed back in the direction they had just come from, towards the prison. The RUC followed. Their plan had been to get to Moira, and now they thought it a good idea to go in another direction. The RUC followed behind them for a few minutes. The men in the car were wearing warders' uniforms. Suddenly, the RUC pulled off to the left and took the Belfast Road. McKearney did a handbreak turn on the road and headed back towards Moira. They stopped in another small town. One of the men jumped out and stopped a man walking along the street.

'Are you a Taig? [Catholic]' he enquired.

'Who the hell are you?' the man asked back.

He was being confronted by a man in a uniform on a Sunday afternoon asking if he was a Taig. The escaper in the uniform started to beg. 'Give us a break,' he asked, 'We're after getting out of the prison.' He took them to his father's house. One man went off to look for the local IRA. They waited for twenty minutes and then a second man disappeared to look for the first. A third man went to look for the first two and the fourth man was left sitting in an empty house. A young woman came in. Was he looking for his friends? He was. They were next door. Tea and sandwiches were being made. One old man in the kitchen told the escapees to 'put your coats on and we'll go for a drink'. After a short while, they were taken to another house. Then other people started to arrive.

Another car with four more in it had arrived in the same town. One man had got out and started to look for the IRA. He disappeared leaving the other three in the car. They could hear the helicopters starting to move around. They grabbed the numberplates off the car and dumped them. Then one of them stopped a woman on the street. 'Are you a nationalist?' he asked. She brought them back to her own house. After a short time, neighbours started to pile into the house. One of the escapers started to panic. All he wanted was to get to a safe house and now the entire neighbourhood seemed to be knocking on the door. 'Get me out of here,' he shouted. He was worried about the car, that it could be identified, but the local IRA had taken the car away. It was being cut into pieces. It was going to end up in the bottom of Lough Neagh. One old woman came in and she started to give rosary beads to the escapees. Twenty-pound notes were being shoved into their pockets. They weren't interested. They were sweating badly and they needed fresh clothes and a safe house. They were moved.

They were sitting in the house, listening to the news, when the doorbell went. Two more escapees. The owner of the house didn't seem perturbed at having six of the most wanted men in the North in his home. He pointed to a shotgun in the corner of the kitchen in the event of any trouble. Then the doorbell went again and two more escapees arrived. Eight. It was getting crowded. Panic started to set in. The eight elected an OC. They told the IRA what they wanted. They wanted transport across the border. They were told that they couldn't move, that there were roadblocks and searches taking place across the North. Every place was being raided. They would have to stay put in the safest house the IRA could arrange in the area. They would have to stay where they were until things cooled off. They were shown where they were going to sleep. It was under the floorboards. They cleared away spaces. There were two groups of four men under there, just below the living-room. It was very cramped. They could lie on their sides, but they didn't sleep well. Every now and then, they would doze off, and then wake up with a start when they realised where they were. They didn't feel safe, but they didn't have any choice. The second group of eight weren't faring much better.

Bik McFarlane and Seamus McElwaine were among the second group. They had commandeered a big green Mercedes. They had headed towards Belfast when rows started about where they were going. Again, people didn't know where the safest place was. They turned their car around and started to head back towards the jail. They drove towards Moira and turned off the main road, sticking to small country lanes. They would have to ditch the car. The police and army knew they were driving it by now. They decided to take over a house. The house they chose belonged to Protestants Ian and Doreen McFarlane. It was near Dromore. Two escapees went in the back door to take it. The Mercedes was driven into the back a few minutes later. The escapers told the McFarlanes that they would leave as soon as possible and that if they did as they were told everything would be all right. Ian McFarlane was nervous. The escapees took a fridge and some cupboards from the front sitting-room and shifted them out to the back. They dumped the stuff in front of the car in an outhouse so that it wouldn't be spotted from the air. Some of the escapees took up positions at the windows and it dawned on them that they were only a short distance from the jail. Others of the escapees had, meanwhile, managed to get within twenty miles of the border. They also realised that they might be within the circle of roadblocks. As it happened, they were just outside the three-mile cordon.

They were between five and seven miles from the jail.

No patrols of British Army or RUC came down the road. Ian McFarlane was a quantity surveyor and a customer was due to call that night to collect some maps. When he finally did call, Doreen McFarlane said he was not at home. He collected his maps and left. But now the escapees had a problem. If they left the McFarlane household they had no way of knowing whether or not the family would go to the police immediately and pin-point where they were. The escapees told the family that the only way they could ensure that this would not happen was to take one of the children hostage—either twelve-year-old Neil or fourteen-year-old Alan. They could also leave one escaper behind instead. The escapees got the family to swear on the Bible that they would not go to the RUC for three days after they left the house, if they took no hostage with them. Bik McFarlane changed into his namesake's clothing. The two young McFarlanes were in the Boy Scouts, and the escapees decided to gather up some of their materials: a compass, a pocket torch, maps of the area, haversacks full of cheese and soda and potato bread, a digital clock and hot water bottles full of water. The telephone and a CB radio in the house were put out of action. Bik McFarlane gave them a signed inventory of every-thing they had taken, and said they could get recompense from the republican movement. The eight men moved out at eleven that night, around the same time as the floorboard gang were clearing space for themselves. The McFarlane family had gone to bed an hour earlier.

A thick fog had come down and it dimmed the lights from the helicopters. The eight walked along the main road at first, diving into a ditch whenever a car would come along. After a couple of miles, they stopped in a field to work out exactly where they wanted to go. They had been running and they lay down to rest. Two British Army or UDR jeeps passed them in the night. They started to walk, through narrow country roads. One man injured his leg and they had to stop to bandage him up. He thought his leg was broken. They used a first aid kit they had taken from the house to deal with it. But the delay cost them valuable time. The injured man couldn't walk properly and had to be helped.

It was coming up to six on the Monday morning when they came across a place which looked safe to spend the daylight hours. They had decided to travel only by night. Two escapees went up ahead to check out the place. In the clump of bushes they slept in fours, side by side for body heat, while the remaining four stood watch. They had one major advantage. Seamus McElwaine knew country areas like the back of his hand. He had lived in the fields and hills. Their idea was to walk the length of the North to the border, avoiding the checkpoints and helicopters. As they started to sleep, the men under the floorboards were waking up.

10

To the Border

The fact that a fifty-strong unit of the IRA managed to get away from within ten miles of the prison following the escape would seem to indicate that if the escapees had made it to that point they would have all got clear. Some of the fleeing escapees in the red Ford passed part of that unit, but had no idea they were behind the ditch. Members of the unit noted the car but didn't pay too much heed to it. When the news began to come across the radio the unit decided it was time to beat a retreat.

British Prime Minister Margaret Thatcher was on an official visit to Canada when she was told about events in the prison. She called the escape 'the gravest in our prison history'. On the Monday morning, Sir James Hennessy, Chief Inspector of Prisons, was flown to the North to look into the escape. His brief was to find out what had happened but, more importantly, how it had happened. And on the same day, Secretary for State for Northern Ireland, James Prior had the following to say:

> When you have a vast number of life prisoners, all very desperate men, a lot of rotten eggs in one basket, there is always great difficulty in controlling them. . . . These men will be on the run, they will be hunted down whether they are in the north of the island or the south of the island, and we shall be doing all we can, in co-operation with the Republic of Ireland, to see that they are recaptured.

The *Belfast Telegraph* in an editorial said that 'in all Ireland, they [the escapees] will find no hiding place'. There were roadblocks on both sides of the border. The understanding was that if any of them were caught they would be handed back to the prison authorities. But at least some of the escapees had found a hiding place. Others were not finding it so easy.

Constable William Ingram was stationed at Castlewellan in County Down. He got a phone call to say that there were two suspicious-looking men on the Clonvaraghan Road, five or six miles outside the town. Ingram and Sergeant McDougall got into their patrol car and headed out the road. One of the scruffy-looking characters was carrying a fork over his shoulder, the other man had a black eye. Ingram asked them what they were doing in the area. They were cleaning out barns, it seemed, and they were from Downpatrick. Ingram wasn't too happy with their answers and invited the two to accompany him back to the station. It was now about 9.30 pm. Paul Kane and Brendan Mead, late of the prison down the road, got into the back of the car.

They had used the fork for pulling each other over ditches. They had been in a car after getting away, but it had broken down after only twenty minutes, and so they had started to wander on foot. They had met men in a field at one stage, and they told the men that they were UVF men and that they were after breaking out of jail. One of the men in the field had passed a remark about Brendan being an unlikely name for a UVF man (Mead had this name tattooed across his arm). The two escapees then told the truth. The men in the field had kept a lookout while the two had a smoke in a nearby ditch. They asked directions for Dromore and then took off for Castlewellan. Then Ingram and McDougall caught up with them.

Anne Cadwallader spent the entire day going around to the locals and talking to them. They told her how frightened they had been, and how they knew that there would be an escape from the prison sooner or later. Earlier that Monday morning the heavy security presence began to pull further and further away from the prison as the net for the men on the run extended. The few miles from the prison to Belfast took at least two hours. The roadblocks were still very heavy. The story was also moving. The reports said that the British and Irish Armies, and the RUC and gardai were co-operating in ways never before seen. Cadwallader wondered how this co-operation was working. Were they back-to-back on border roads, for example, or were the forces of each side blocking off alternative roads. She drove down to the border, crossed it ten times between Newry and Crossmaglen, on both main and unapproved roads. She wasn't stopped once. The co-operation in that area at least was non-existent.

Escaper Kevin Barry Artt had got stranded on his own. As soon as he got to the field, he had gone into a house close to the prison and stayed there for a while. A British Army patrol went by, but didn't go in. He started to walk to Belfast on foot, passed through three checkpoints and was stopped at one of them. He was allowed through. He managed to get as far as Andersonstown, in West Belfast. Eventually he would be brought across the border.

Under the floorboards that morning the eight began to take stock of their situation. Dust and rubble and stones were everywhere and now they began to clear away spaces properly. It wasn't possible to sit up in the spaces, measuring between twelve and eighteen inches, but they could turn on their sides and change position every now and then. The owners of the house appeared very calm to the escapees. The woman was eight months pregnant. She had made a big pot of stew for the men that first night. They had listened to the television news under the boards. Covered in coats and blankets they had tried to sleep. Then on the Monday, they began to get the news of those who had been caught. The radio was giving out the details as soon as they became available. This was of some help to those who were still free, since they were getting an idea of where the searches were being concentrated, and could take steps, if possible, to avoid those areas. Some of the men weren't sure if the reports were accurate, or if the reports weren't an RUC ploy to get them to make a mistake.

A light was put in under the boards. When the light was on, it meant that the men could talk. When the light was off it meant that there were visitors and they were to keep quiet. Since they could hear the radio and television from under the boards it followed that whatever they said could be heard in the living-room.

A coffee jar was used as a toilet. It was passed in and out to the men on the inside. The jar was filled into a bucket and emptied as soon as it was full. If they needed to move their bowels they could go upstairs, but it was dangerous. They got newspapers on the first day and read accounts of what had happened. They tended to believe the reports of the searches moving away from their area. It was good news for the men under the boards. It wasn't such good news for others.

Patrick McIntyre and Joe Corey had moved to just such an

area. They were in County Down, twenty-five miles from the prison. They had got there late, heard the radio and television news, and contacted the local IRA. They could hear what was happening on Monday. They heard about Mead and Kane later that day, but didn't at that stage know their identities. The searches started to move towards Downpatrick. The two men could hear the choppers and the spotter planes moving farther and farther away. McIntyre and Carey knew there were points in their area. Hearing the reports of people getting caught they wondered how they would react if the RUC caught them. Would they make a run for it? Would they surrender? They were holed up in an attic.

The eight men in the countryside all came awake around three in the afternoon. They were exhausted. They breakfasted on chocolate bars and soda bread. They knew from the radio that seven of the thirty-eight had been caught. They started to talk. They came to the view that if they were caught in the fields they would be shot dead on sight, they would not be given a chance to surrender. As one remarked, 'it would have suited them to take us out of the game'. It was around nine that night when they moved off, picking up all their rubbish. They were still sticking to the roads. When a car came along they jumped into the ditch, no matter what particular hazards might be at the spot they found themselves jumping across. Men fell into gripes and cut themselves. They could hear the helicopters sometimes, and there were roadblocks. It wasn't long before they ran out of food. It was a clear night and they used the compass they had taken off the young McFarlane to travel, and the North Star. But they still took a number of wrong directions.

The atmosphere wasn't too good at times. They could see the RUC patrols passing them. Some of the men were sick and they were shivering with the cold and totally exhausted. Seamus McElwaine wasn't making himself very popular either; some of the men wanted to take over a house but McElwaine objected. It was too dangerous.

The eight under the floorboards were still talking about the escape, and what part each had played in it. The first night under there had presented them with a major problem: someone was snoring very loudly. There was a vent under the boards which led onto the street and they were afraid that somebody passing by might be able to hear it. Someone was going to have

113

to keep watch to find out who the snorer was, and keep him awake. McKearney eventually found out that it was Derryman Kieran Fleming, and so somebody had to stay awake with Fleming all night.

On the Tuesday, McIntyre and Corey ran out of luck. Things were quiet where they were, but there were still checkpoints and roadblocks. They had made up their minds that they were leaving the house as soon as it got dark. They could hear the sound of the odd car passing. Then one of them suddenly noticed that there were no cars passing any more. Everything had gone silent. There was nothing moving.

They could hear the sound of sirens and dogs. Listening, McIntyre thought he heard a voice saying something like 'I've got you covered, Billy.' The sound of doors slamming and shouting came to the two men. 'Come on out, we know you're in there' was the next voice they heard, through a loud hailer. McIntyre looked out the bathroom window. There was a hill at the back. All he could see were scores and scores of RUC men with guns pointed at the house. A person from next door came in to see McIntyre to say there was a phone call. McIntyre walked the gauntlet of RUC men to the next house. The man in charge of the security operation was on the phone. McIntyre wanted a priest and a member of the republican movement present when he surrendered. McIntyre said there was no need to panic. The two escapees would be taken to Newcastle RUC station, they were told. Walking back to the house, McIntyre had a vision of hundreds of RUC men. There was a circle of RUC men, and outside that again, there was another circle of British Army and UDR men. In between, there were six men in plain clothes who looked very sinister at that time. They stood there and stared and made no move. The entire area was covered in jeeps and saracens.

The two men gave themselves up and were placed lying on the ground. They made a comment about the cameras that were taking shots, and were told that they were RUC cameras, for internal use. Later, the same pictures were beamed out on television. They were taken to Newcastle and later to Castlereagh Interrogation Centre. They were brought in what looked like a horse box, with separate cubicles for each man. In the cell in Castlereagh McIntyre could hear mumbling. He called out and asked who was there. 'Gerry' came the reply. 'Gerry from where?' he asked. 'Gerry from H7' came the doleful answer.

Meanwhile, Padraig McKearney was keeping the conversation flowing under the boards. He was a political thinker and started talking about where the movement was going. He was especially forthcoming about what he termed the 'strategic defensive', the 'third phase of the struggle'. This involved holding small areas of support and depriving the RUC, UDR and British Army of a presence in these areas. But eight men living in such close proximity began to get on each other's nerves. They veered between elation at being free, and depression at the thought that they might get caught. Some of the men wanted to talk while others just wanted to be left alone. One man began to recount how he had been arrested one morning. He was in the back of a jeep on his way to Gough barracks for interrogation. The jeep pulled up at traffic lights. Alongside the jeep, a car pulled up, driven by what appeared to be a businessman on his way to work. It crossed the mind of the prisoner how easy it would have been for the two men to be in each other's places. How easy it would have been for the prisoner to be on his way to work; how easy for the businessman to be on his way to Gough barracks. A changed decision here, a different circumstance there.

They got into long talks and debates about the movement, where it was going, the leadership, the personalities. Then they would panic again when they realised how vulnerable they were. Even the most ardent atheists started to pray. Padraig McKearney refused to join in, he informed his friends that it was a well-known fact that there was no such thing as God. The IRA Army Council sent in their 'heartiest congratulations' to the men. It was supposed to be a morale booster, but they weren't interested. They wanted out from under the floorboards. Depression started to set in as they realised that they were going to be under those boards for at least a week. Here they were—they had escaped but they weren't free at all.

The eight men in the countryside were on the move again. They were in a field, walking close to the road. Heavy fog had come down and visibility was down to about twenty feet. They heard a noise. Everybody, travelling in single file military formation, stopped. After a few moments a horse emerged out of the fog. They were travelling through horse-rearing country all the time. But they were as likely to bump into an SAS unit. They

115

had very few weapons, only a shortarm, and by now they were tired and sore.

They had arrived at Gilford and had circled around the town. They were close to the Bann River and needed to cross it, but they couldn't find a suitable ford. They were scared. And then they came to a manor house. They found an old orchard nearby, with apples rotting on the ground and they started to collect them up. They came to some thick undergrowth but couldn't get past the manor house. They moved further into the estate and arrived at a greenhouse. There was a large overflowing tree on a slope nearby. They made up a bed of leaves and used their coats for blankets, then they took turns at sleeping and keeping watch, two hours for each. They were still in the bushes when they heard the noise.

In the morning, a man and a woman had gone into the greenhouse for a few minutes. Later in the day, a man with a dog also went in for a while. The man had an English accent and the black labrador kept coming over to the bushes and barking. His owner dragged him away, but the black dog came back again, with two more dogs in tow. Fifteen minutes later, an RUC patrol pulled up in the driveway. An RUC man got out and everybody underneath the tree started to groan. They were in no mood to start running. They got their shoes and socks on. Then two more RUC men started to walk around. The first RUC man came to within twenty yards of the bushes and stopped. He stared at the bushes. Nobody moved. All eight were sure they had been seen. The RUC man just stayed for about five minutes, smoking a cigarette and staring at the bushes. He stubbed out the cigarette and walked back to the police car. The eight men started to crawl through the undergrowth on their bellies. They crawled for hours and made their way through the estate. They were ripped and torn by brambles and bushes and thorns. They finally came to a laneway where they found some berries and ate them. Two boys with fishing rods passed, saw two of the escapees and took to their heels. They then waded through the fast-flowing river Bann and climbed up the hill which overlooked the area. It was late that evening when they took cover again and they waited until the darkness fell before moving further southwards.

They came to Scarva at last. They were feeling very down and some of the eight wanted to take over a house. They watched a house where the family had visitors. The visitors left around midnight and the owner of the house went around checking all his doors and windows. The men in the darkness wanted to take the house badly, get some hot food and tobacco, get some sleep. But McElwaine wasn't happy about the set-up; the owner checking all the doors and windows gave him a bad feeling. If they took the house, they would be starting a fresh trail and giving the police and army new clues as to where they were. By now, they were sure that the McFarlane family had kept their word and hadn't gone to the police. In fact, the McFarlanes weren't too sure what they were going to do. Eventually they went to a clergyman and asked his advice. They were advised to follow their conscience.

Bik McFarlane had about £1.50 left in his pocket. He decided that it would be a good idea to phone a safe house in Belfast to try and get some help, but then he changed his mind. Telephone taps would give away their location. They moved on through the night, came to Poyntz Pass and then they saw a signpost for Newry, ten miles away. The nearness of Newry gave them fresh heart and they gathered speed. They took to the main road, wanting to get as many miles as possible behind them. When the dawn come up, they were on top of a small hill in a thicket bush. They had neither food nor water.

It was Wednesday night when they started off again, heading south-west. Near Newry, they came across the railway line and cut off to one side to avoid the town. They used the railway line as a guide and then took to the fields. They were in very high spirits by now, sure that they were going to make it, and they pushed themselves onwards. They had cut off the railway track and weren't too sure where they were. Then they came to three houses and the men wanted to take one of them over, but again McElwaine was against it. There were dogs at one of the houses, and they kept barking. Seven of the eight lay down on the roadside from pure exhaustion. Some were on the grass and there were one or two just lying across walls on the side of the road. The eighth went to check out the farmhouse. He came back after a few minutes. It seemed all right. They would be able to sleep in the barn. And then the last apple from the orchard was produced. It was partly rotten. The rotten parts were cut away, and it was divided in to eight pieces. That was supper. They settled into the barn for the night.

The men under the floorboards seemed to be using the toilet more often than was necessary. Each journey represented a risk, and if the journey was unnecessary, so was the risk. They began to count how often each man went upstairs. It didn't help morale. On one occasion one of the escapees was half lying, half raised, on his way out to the toilet. Suddenly the light went out. He had to freeze, but he was in such an awkward position, he shifted to get comfortable. Wham! He hit a beam with his leg and the noise reverberated through the house. The whispering started under the boards. 'Who was that?' And overhead, they could hear the voice of a young boy saying that he could hear whispering. The woman went upstairs to check. She thought there might be something up there. She came back a few minutes later. A window had fallen down, she said.

And then they started to stink. The woman could smell the men from the living-room. She asked for the eight to send their socks up so that they could be washed. But it didn't make the smell go away. They were afraid that a British Army patrol with dogs would stop at the vent and that the dog would give their location away. So they sent out for dog spray normally used on bitches in heat. They thought that if they sprayed it on the vent, it would give them immunity from curious dogs. They were putting it on when a gust of wind blew the spray back under the boards. The men were gasping and choking. And then the word came that they were to be moved, in twos.

Back in the countryside the trekking gang were waking up. They watched the farmhouse as two men left for work. Then one of them approached the house. They asked the woman would she make some tea. She would. Then they all trooped into the house and drank a cup of tea for the first time in four days. They also smoked their brains out. They'd had very little tobacco. And they ate and ate. From there they made contact with the local IRA. Later that evening they were collected and dropped off close to the border. They had to wait throughout the night in no-man's land.

On the Friday morning, as they waited, newspapers were brought to them, and anything else they required. Armed IRA men and women were guarding them and the pressure was off them for the first time. They read about the escape in the newspapers. One of the eight thought about sueing an English newspaper for a particularly unflattering photograph they published of him. Another threatened to contact the same paper for putting his age down as thirty-eight rather than twenty-eight. They were very high. The escape was a joke to them now. At 1 am, they crossed the border. They were supposed to wait close to the border, in the fields, but they decided to walk the last few miles to a safe house. When they came to the last obstacle in the North, a gate at the end of a field, one of the armed IRA men insisted in kicking the gate down. They moved southwards.

Padraig McKearney was the first man out from under the boards. The men had lived there for two weeks. They were filthy and the growth on their faces was twice that it normally would have been, due possibly to the heat. Their legs were very weak. One took a bath, while another shaved, while another sat on the toilet. The same bathwater was used for all eight as the plughole exit was on the outside of the house and too much water might be noticed, especially if it were black.

A man in the house handed McKearney a 'grenade' before he left the house. 'Take this,' he was told, 'it might come in useful if you run into trouble.' McKearney was delighted, and was hopping the 'grenade' up and down in his hands. He was disappointed to discover that it was nothing more than a cigarette lighter. None of these escapees were armed. McKearney was moved out first, with another of the eight. A red Ford Escort was used and there was an IRA scout car in front and behind. It would take them another two weeks to cross the border. Some of the escapees had their hair dyed and then they were all debriefed. At one point, there were two IRA people debriefing an escaper in an upstairs bedroom. A knock came to the door. It was the RUC. They were looking for a previous owner. The escapees were moved again.

It was in the dark that they finally moved towards the border, back into South Armagh. The IRA used CBs to communicate with each other. Some of the escapees got delayed and didn't make it to the pick-up point. The message went out across the radio to the unit waiting up the road: 'We're on our way with half our cargo.'

Local armed units of the IRA stood out at crossroads to welcome the men. In the darkness the escapees could hear the blades of a British helicopter. They were worried, but they were told not to worry, there were no British troops on the ground in the area. In South Armagh, the escapees were brought from

119

house to house. More rosary beads and money were heaped upon them. An old man gave one of them an old .45 pistol. 'Here,' he said, 'never mind the rosaries, put this in your pocket.' And then they all entered a total security freeze.

They were not to do anything for a period of time. They were taken offside. Those that had not already been debriefed now underwent rigorous questioning. They had to relate their part in the escape and what exactly they had done. Then they were offered options. They were asked what part, if any, they wanted to play within the republican movement. They were asked if they wished to leave the country for a while. Some took up this option, some opted out of the republican movement altogether. None of them were allowed to return to active service immediately. They needed to sort themselves out mentally and physically. All they had to do was follow orders. There were nineteen men of the thirty-eight still free. They were dispersed North and South.

11

Aftermath

The IRA refuses to be drawn on how the weapons were taken into the prison except to point out that there were many different routes through which the weapons could have come. In fact, the options were fairly extensive. But there was also a quantity of other stuff which the Provos had managed to get into the prison, or at least hide. This was found as soon as the searches started.

The gardens around the prison were dug and other implements of escape were found, among them ladders and ropes. Some of the equipment had been gathered together by the men who had been ordered to stop their escape. And Sir James Hennessy, the Chief Inspector for Prisons for England and Wales, had some unflattering things to say about the prison and its security.

His terms of reference had been 'to conduct an Inquiry into the security arrangements at HM Prison Maze relative to the escape on Sunday 25 September 1983 and to make relevant recommendations for the improvement of security at HM Prison, Maze.'

His Deputy took part in the inquiry, as did two former Governors, a former Administration Officer and two Chief Officers. Two days after the escape he set up office at the prison and stayed there for almost five weeks. He examined the physical layout of the Blocks, the routines and the procedures. He sent a letter to every employee at the prison who had been on duty the day of the escape, or whose duties concerned security. He interviewed 115 members of staff, or former members. He also invited prisoners to give evidence and twenty-eight responded in writing. In his introduction Sir James noted that there were serious allegations made against prison staff, and that if these allegations were proved, they 'involved the commission of criminal offences'. He left the RUC to follow up the allegations of beatings. The Report was published in January 1984, just four months after the escape.

In making his Report he said he tried to avoid making recommendations with the benefit of hindsight. 'On every important issue', he said, 'we have tried to judge whether the actions taken by those concerned were reasonable in the light of the information available to them and in the circumstances prevailing at the time.'

He outlined a short history of the prison, the prisoners and the prison department. He gave a racy account of the takeover of H-Block 7 and of the actual escape itself. He was able to piece together the sequence of events fairly accurately, given the fact that he did not have the co-operation of those who were involved in the escape. He referred to the escape as being 'audacious and daring'. And viewed in light of the fact that the prison was supposed to be one of the most secure in the North the escape 'must be judged the most serious escape in recent history of the United Kingdom Prison Services'. In fact, it was the largest breakout since the Second World War.

Sir James traced the history of the blanket protest, the ending of all protests, the appointment of lifers as orderlies, the manipulation of the prison warders. He noted that orderly posts represented a threat to security and that those posts should be confined to a minimum in number 'consistent with good housekeeping'. The workshops, which at one time also represented a similar threat, had been closed immediately after the escape. The Provos had therefore achieved their fifth and final demand of the hunger strikers—no work.

Sir James recommended that information on the prison should be collated, so that patterns, such as the pattern of a decrease in the number of incidents as had occurred in H7 just prior to the breakout, should be noticed. Searches on visits should be tightened up, he said, as should vehicle checks and staff vetting. He was unable to state by which route the weapons had come in but noted the supply lorries, the visiting area and other ways they could have come in. He conceded that body searches of visitors would have to be introduced to stop the possibility of any weapons ever getting in again. (Body frisking was already going on.) He stopped short of recommending this. 'In the end we believe that this is a matter for the government of the day to judge in the light of the security situation in Northern Ireland. If the government judges that despite the safeguards we have recommended, the remaining risks to security at the Maze—and by extension to law and order in Northern Ireland—are unacceptable, then stricter measures may have to be taken.'

He also recommended a tightening-up on searches in the Blocks, the installation of TV monitors, the introduction of codewords, improved alarm and communication links, reinforcing of the gates and the locks, securing of the armoury, and so on. But along with improving the purely technical aspects of security, he also spotted the same flaws that Papillon had spotted—the potential to exploit human weakness. He made sweeping recommendations in relation to the vetting of staff and how they might be kept on their toes. The establishment of a Quick Reaction Force was urged. He was slightly critical of the soldier who had shot Harry 'The Crab' Murray. He took the view that the soldier could have fired his baton gun, or CS gas, or he could have let go with the rifle a bit more. 'It is possible that more prisoners would have been prevented from escaping' he said, had this happened. A review of the orders under which British soldiers are legally entitled to fire their weapons was urged.

Sir James next turned his attention to the plans that had been put into operation by the RUC and UDR and British Army that day, namely their setting-up of vehicle checkpoints under Operation Vesper. The RUC had three up by 4.25 pm, and three escapees were caught in two separate roadblocks as a result. But he had criticisms. The RUC had no photographs of the men they were looking for. He recommended that they should get photographs much quicker in the event of the same thing happening again.

The alarm had been raised at 4.12 pm that day, and two minutes later the RUC and British Army had started to throw up roadblocks. Hennessy noted that most of the escapees had got away before the first cordon was in place around the prison. The cordon, in any event, was primarily designed to thwart an attack on the prison from the outside, not to stop an escape. The vehicle checkpoints had been in place within thirteen minutes. In those thirteen minutes, a man could run two miles, or drive ten miles. The cordons were sited between one half and two miles from the prison. Hennessy thought they should be resited.

He was critical of staff who had become lax in their duties. Security gates had been left open, prisoners weren't searched, posts were left unattended, vehicles weren't searched. He noted that standards had fallen as the size of the prison service had grown. It had increased tenfold since the early seventies. More vetting and more training and less sloppy practices were recommended. Leaving early on Sunday afternoons should cease. The general efficiency of prison officers and warders and their superiors should be increased. 'At all levels', he said, 'the quality of managerial control, direction and leadership proved inadequate.'

Sir James also came across a report that had been made on the prison as far back as 1978, carried out by the RUC and commissioned by the Penal Department. It had been made against the background of the possibility of an escape, and it contained 101 recommendations, 71 of which had been complied with, either fully or in part. However, the Prison Department appeared to be unaware of the report when Sir James went looking for it in 1983.

Sir James also recommended a change in the type of work prisoners should do. The traditional workshops had given them movement and access to weapons. That had to change.

The prison budget for 1983 was almost £70 million. There were more than 3,000 staff. The prison service had never been refused any reasonable request for money or extra resources. The inference could be drawn from that that there was no shortage of money to keep the prisoners in the jails.

Hennessy acknowledged the special circumstances in the North. He said that the prison population consisted 'almost entirely of prisoners convicted of offences connected with terrorist activities, united in their determination to be treated as political prisoners, resisting prison discipline, even if it means starving themselves to death, and retaining their paramilitary structure and allegiances even when inside'. And then he ended his report as follows:

> This [Report] will not solve all the problems of the Maze: tensions can be expected to continue as long as the troubles in Northern Ireland continue. Nor will it guarantee security—no prison is ever more secure than the weakest member of its staff—and absolute security can never be

guaranteed without resort to inhuman and unacceptable methods. But with inspired leadership and proper support, the prison should soon become again what it always was intended to be; the most secure prison in Northern Ireland.

The names of all the staff, with the exception of James Ferris who had been killed, were deleted from the report, for security reasons. The drawings of the main gate and the Visitors Complex were deleted from the report for the same reasons.

In October 1983 the Escape Committee within the prison was back at the drawing board. They were again starting from scratch. Many of the routes for supplies and messages had been closed off in the immediate aftermath of the escape. There were more ideas coming forward. Papillon felt that they could have one more crack at the prison before security was closed off completely. While the prison authorities were closing off various avenues and routes they were by no means shutting off everything.

The IRA on the outside would be involved again. Things were looking up on that front too. Robert Lean had been moved from one place to another throughout the North. A week after the escape, his wife left the custody of the police and returned home. Lean stayed with the police. But two weeks later he decided to move.

He was being held in Palace barracks and the security around him had been relaxed somewhat. One of his 'minders' had left his car keys on a mantelpiece in a room and gone off to bed. It was just half an hour after midnight on 19 October. Lean took a shave, grabbed the keys, climbed through the window and drove out of the barracks.

The following day, he turned up at a press conference at the Felon's Club in West Belfast. He was flanked by members of the leadership of Sinn Féin. Lean said he had been offered money to finger top people within the movement. He said he was a member of Sinn Féin but not the IRA. As he left the Club following the conference he was arrested. His retraction was the fourth in a month and it heralded the beginning of the end of the informer system. It had been used successfully as a weapon for a period of two years. It had brought the courts into disrepute and wrought havoc to both nationalist and loyalist communities during that time.

The Escape Committee had much information on the prison

which was still valid. And in everyday conversation the warders were telling the prisoners where they had gone wrong. The warders were convinced that such an escape could never happen again. Then came the Hennessy Report on the prison. This told the Provos a lot they didn't know before—such as the reaction force. As a result of the report, the Escape Committee had a much better idea of when to time an escape.

There were cameras and monitors in all the Circles of the Blocks, and at the front gate. The gates were electronically controlled. There were posters all over the Blocks with the 'Five Golden Rules' written up. No prisoners were to go anywhere without an escort. No prisoner was to go anywhere without a valid reason. No prisoner was to move anywhere without that move being documented. A new lease of life was being injected into the warders. The workshops were gone, and football, and the gym. But there were still visits and the hospital. There some movement. Papillon was still plotting away.

The original idea had been to take the Administration Block, the security nerve centre. If they could take that, it wouldn't matter how many alarms were pressed. There was only one entrance to the Emergency Control Room (the ECR), located in the Admin Block. Another warder was 'turned up'. He was a gambler. He knew all the finer details about the Admin Block from having worked there. He knew about the night guard, the procedures that were used. Papillon asked a prisoner who knew him well to make overtures to him. The warder said he would only deal with the top man. Papillon and the warder started to talk to each other. The warder wanted a lot of money. He wanted £10,000. No problem. He got about £300 as a down payment, with the promise of the rest when the escape was over. He gave them enough information to reach the ECR. He knew that he was helping the Provos plan an escape, which if it was successful would make September 1983 look like a tea party.

Papillon began to develop the plan. A prisoner would get sick and would go to the medical orderly. A van would be brought up to bring the sick man to hospital. The van would then be hijacked. The hospital was just beside the ECR. The ECR would be taken from there. Having taken the ECR, the Provos would then have total control of the jail.

Around 6 am every morning the gates were opened; they were usually closed all night. A diversion, such as a major fire, would be started. A fire had already been started to time how long it would take the fire engines to reach the prison. Then they would take off. There would be up to 300 people going out this time. Even though there were twice that number in jail, many had short sentences left to serve and the risk of escaping and getting caught wasn't worth it.

Again, there would be a pick-up point close to the jail. They would be met by armed action service units and the entire unit would travel back into South Armagh. Safe houses would have to be set up all over the island. It was more or less the same plan as before, except that the number of men leaving would be ten times greater.

There were plenty of vans and cars at the Tally Lodge and about twenty would be hijacked. Christmas 1984 was set as a provisional date for the escape. The time of year would give cover of darkness for the escapees. By August 1984 a specific date had not been set. The warder was still meeting with Provos on the outside. For whatever reason he was picked up by the RUC and interrogated. He cracked and told the RUC what he had done. He got three years in jail and the escape plan was off. But the men in jail didn't stop looking for a way out.

It took months for the Blocks to get back to normal. For about three months the warders obeyed every directive to the letter, but by the start of 1984 they were less rigorous about applying too strict an interpretation to the rules.

New warders were recruited and some of them came from the UDR and British Army. Such men were likely to be less susceptible to the wooing of the prisoners. Some of the warders who had been working on the day of the escape tried to maintain a very strict discipline on the prisoners. It was as if they were trying to redeem themselves. The Provos informed them that if they didn't ease up there would be trouble.

Some of the hardline officers, who had been shunted aside when the blanket men were coming off their protests, were now promoted. The thinking seemed to be that the softly-softly approach hadn't worked and now it was time to try something else. There were three such officers in senior positions. A senior officer appeared at a staff parade in the Circle of H7 early in 1984. He told the warders that they were fighting an army and that the warders themselves would have to behave like an army. He epitomised the hardline approach.

A prison officer appeared in silhouette on television in early 1984. He said that it was necessary to integrate all loyalist and republican prisoners as a matter of priority. There was a section within the prison service who subscribed to this line of thought. The Provos identified the three main men in what they took to be an assault on themselves. The Provos had been trying to find out who was pushing the new integration policy. Eventually they found out who it was. He appeared to be coming more and more into the picture and looked as if he was going to be promoted. The consequences for life within the prison could be very serious.

The officer seemed to want to show that he could be a trouble-shooter and that he knew how to be tough with the Provos. It was late February 1984 when the forced integration started. The officer received death threats, he ignored them. The warders on the inside were told by the Provos that if he pushed integration he would be shot dead. The warders were advised not to proceed with the plans for integration. They were called in by the officer and told that they would have to implement the new policy. The warders went back to the Provos. The Provos told them to forget about it, to go ahead and do whatever they had to do. Two days later the officer was shot dead.

The morning he was killed the prison authorities sent for the Provo spokesman within the jail. The authorities wanted to know if there was a change of policy, were prison officers now going to be killed? Were they back to the hunger strikes' scenario? No. There was no change in policy. The Provos pointed out that there were five lifers on each Wing, and that if they wanted to kill prison officers within the jail they could do that. The authorities decided that enough was enough. Integration wasn't pushed. Four weeks later life began to return to normal.

At the time of writing there are still up to forty claims outstanding against the Secretary of State for Northern Ireland and the Governor of the prison for alleged assaults on prisoners during the follow-up searches after the escape. One claim found a resolution in the High Court in Belfast in October 1987. The Court found that while the prisoner who took the action had not been beaten he was entitled to compensation for damage to personal property which had been completely destroyed during those searches.

Mr Justice MacDermott said there was a conflict of evidence as to whether the prisoner had been beaten, and that his conflict could sometimes be resolved by looking at the medical evidence. But the prisoner had not been seen by a doctor until nine days after he said he was beaten and the evidence was therefore of limited value in determining where the truth of the matter lay.

The prisoner's cell door had been opened at five that afternoon. A frisk search was carried out, which only took a matter of a few seconds. Three hours later, the prisoner was strip searched. The cell was given a thorough search. Warders came back later and asked him to strip again but they left after he had started to take off his clothes. The prisoner said that he had been told that there would be no medical visits for three days following the escape. The medical evidence was not proof enough to back up the claims of assault. He was awarded £150 for damaged personal property, plus costs. The other cases have yet to come before the courts, although there have been attempts made to settle them out of court.

There was confusion in those weeks following the escape. There was still the film of the takeover of H-Block 7. The escapees had not brought it with them. It was on a prisoner who had been caught. Following the recapture of nineteen men orders were sent in to destroy the film. Both the camera and the film were hidden on the Boards. The orders got mixed up and both the film and the camera were destroyed.

Derek Carson, State Pathologist for Northern Ireland, examined the body of James Ferris, the prison officer who was stabbed during the escape. He found that he had died of 'acute coronary insufficiency due to coronory atheroma and emotional stress'. He noted a triangular stab wound measuring 9mm by 7mm by 6mm in the right upper abdomen. There was a 4mm wound in the same area. Another wound, 6mm by 2mm, was located on the left side at the back of the chest. One of the wounds had penetrated the body cavity. Derek Carson said that James Ferris had not been 'in good health'. There were scars on his heart from previous heart attacks. 'His heart disease', he noted, 'was of a severity which could have caused sudden collapse and death at any time.' The stab wounds 'had not caused serious internal injury' and that 'in an otherwise healthy individual they should certainly not have caused serious incapacity or death'. He was forty-three years old.

12

Where are they now?

Throughout late September and October, the roadblocks and searches for the missing nineteen men were scaled down. And through those months, they were debriefed by the IRA. The part each man had played in the escape was written down and all were instructed not to talk about it again. Then all were offered options as to what they wanted to do with their lives. While it was true that they had been chosen to go on the escape because of their operational capabilities, and it was hoped that they would remain within the movement, they still had that choice.

Some of the men opted to return to active service, mostly along the border. Others severed their links with the movement, more went abroad. All 'took time out' to adjust to their life on the outside.

The escapees had a curious view of what life on the run in the South would be like. They imagined that they would be able to walk about freely, to go for a drink or to a disco when they felt like it, and pretty much to lead a normal life. It had been a feature of previous escapes that men on the run would turn up in public places. It was also a feature of previous escapes that many were caught. It had occurred to leaders within the IRA that perhaps these two facts were linked. Life would be very different for the men of H-Block 7. If they were caught in the South, they knew they would be handed back by the government.

The men from Belfast and Derry could not go home. They would be recognised immediately if they went back to visit their families and friends. They underwent a period of adjustment, which in some cases took years. There were, of course, furtive meetings with families and loved ones south of the border. But they had to break completely with their past.

Those from the cities that took up the option of returning to active service along the border had a lot to learn, and also much to teach their rural counterparts. Later, people like Seamus McElwaine would show the city men how to live close to the fields, how to live rough for weeks on end, how to cross ditches and drains and fight a war in the countryside. It was a very different proposition to the type of close encounter they had been used to with the RUC and British Army on the narrow and winding streets of Belfast. All of that was to come later, but a couple of months after the escape, nothing had prepared them for this new life. For a start, they were all split up. One particular escapee wanted to get out and about. He was being moved from house to house in the West of Ireland. But the only outings he got were at night, and only then when there was someone there to watch over him. The greatest difficulty was the Northern accent, which was instantly recognisable. Some of the men afterwards took elocution lessons to try and hide their accent. He was living on a farm, and in the early morning, would put on wellingtons and jeans to familiarise himself with the hills and fields of Leitrim. Wearing a heavy coat, he walked through thousands and thousands of acres of young forests. Once a uniformed garda and two plainclothes detectives called to the house where he was staying. He looked on from the nearby fields. Then, large scale sweeps started and it was more difficult not to get caught. He spent the nights sleeping in a hayshed adjoining the house, with dogs for company. They were good. They barked when strangers came and alerted him.

He got up very early and wandered the fields until about 8 am. On Friday 16 December 1983, less than three months after the escape, the routine was no different. He was coming back that morning from his walkabout when he was approached by the man of the house carrying a bale of hay on his back. The news wasn't good. The army and gardai were about, searching. Looking across the hills, he could see row on row of men, moving across the countryside. He ran hard in the opposite direction.

He was short and stocky, and moved through briars and brambles, gaps and drains, mile after mile. Hours of running. Stopping in the centre of a field, he saw a gap at the bottom. By now he was sure he was safe. The only trouble was that he hadn't a clue where he was. Actually he had come circling back almost to where he started. A uniformed garda and two plainclothes detectives moved into the field and saw him. Again he bolted, finally diving into a bush. Except that there was a river on the far side.

Nestling up against the embankment, with weeds hanging down in front, he spotted the garda recruit walking up the far bank. He was sure the man was a recruit because he looked so young. 'Are you all right?' called the recruit. His heart stopped. Then a voice on the bank over his head answered. 'Yeah I'm all right.' By now he was wet and shivering and frightened. The garda walked down again, and then went away. It was around noon and he stayed in the river, counting the minutes and hours away. In the afternoon, there was shooting fairly close by. He hadn't a clue what was happening and decided not to move. He stayed in the river. He was caught up in Operation Santa Claus.

The Operation had been launched three days earlier by the gardai and the army. The army had brought in their crack Rangers for the exercise. Hundreds of men were combing the Leitrim countryside, looking for a kidnapped supermarket executive, Don Tidey. The Provos had taken him from his Dublin home three weeks before and were looking for £5 million for his safe return. From a viewpoint on the Sliabh of Iarainn hills, all you could see was dense young forest covering the countryside. As you moved in closer, that countryside was covered in bramble and briar which was impossible to search. Leitrim can grow forests faster than anywhere else in Europe.

About a mile from Derrada Post Office there was a slight hill. The trees there were no more than a few feet high. For three weeks Don Tidey had been held there. Polythene was stretched about two foot over the ground, between the trees, camouflaged with briars and bushes. It measured 15 foot by 4 foot. The search parties had been split into ten teams, named Rudolph One to Ten. It was around 2 pm when members of Rudolph 5 approached the hideout at Derrada wood.

Hundreds of garda recruits, who had not completed their training, had been drafted in for the search. Gary Sheehan was just such a recruit. He saw in front of him, as he approached the hideout, a figure dressed in army uniform. Despite being spoken to by Sheehan the figure never replied. Sheehan turned to Private Patrick Kelly, who was behind him to make some remark about the strange man who wouldn't say anything to him. The IRA were now trapped, a gun battle started and

132

within a few seconds, Gary Sheehan and Patrick Kelly lay dead. The Provos emerged from the hideout and threw a stun grenade in the direction of the following soldiers and gardai. Then they took three gardai and a soldier hostage and came out of the wood, armed. They knew they were trapped. They took two more soldiers. In the ensuing debacle Don Tidey managed to free himself. He was standing in the roadway, haggard and worn, trying to convince gardai that he was who he said he was. He had three weeks' growth on his face and was wearing combat gear. That was when the blue Opel car came swerving and screeching towards the gardai.

There were five IRA men in the car, two of them in the boot. As they passed the gardai, the men in the boot sprayed gunfire in the general direction of their would-be-captors. Further up the road the word went out fast that the Provos were firing from a blue car. Oblivious to all of this another garda was escorting a man he had just arrested back towards the scene of the action. They were driving in a blue car. The gardai and army opened up. As soon as it was realised what was happening, the word went out to stop firing on the blue car. Finding their way blocked the Provos abandoned their vehicle and headed northwards, looking for the cover of the hills. They moved very quickly through the countryside, giving covering fire to each other as they moved forward one at a time. As they moved further and further away, dusk was starting to come down over Leitrim.

As the kidnappers moved away under cover of darkness, the escapee was emerging from the river. He finally managed to locate a familiar landmark, and crossed the fields back to the house. He got a bath, a hot whiskey, food and a change of clothes and headed for the hayshed for the night. On the Saturday, he constructed a hollowed-out space for himself in the hayshed by removing some bales of hay, but didn't bother to tell the people in this house this. And on the Sunday morning early, the dogs started to bark again.

There were sounds of cars stopping, doors slamming, and voices coming closer. From underneath the hideaway, the voices became clearer and clearer and it was possible to make out what they were saying. The soldiers and gardai could be heard up on top of the hay, searching. Then they moved away.

In the following days the Tidey kidnappers made their way

out of the area. The gardai let it be known that they wished to interview three of the escapees in connection with the shootout at Derrada wood. They were Brendan McFarlane, Tony McAllister and Gerry McDonnell. The Provos denied that any of the escapees were involved. In fact, one escapee was involved. The escapee in the hayshed was moved to another area shortly after that and was moved into a farmhouse with an elderly couple some distance away. Life was different there, not least because Kieran Fleming, another escapee, was there also. The two men started to learn a bit about farming, about how cows gave birth to their young and how to live in the country.

Every now and then the two would get out for a drink. During the day they did work about the farm. At one point a cow was due to calve, and Kieran Fleming didn't know how to broach the subject with the farmer at the breakfast table in front of his wife. The details of the process were embarrassing to him. The two men talked often about what they would do if the 'Taskies' came. They were always expecting the gardai. Kieran Fleming said that he would be well able to get away, no problem. The other man pointed to a gate at the end of a shed, several feet high, and asked him if he would be able to clear it if the Taskies arrived on the spot. Fleming didn't think he would have any problem, and took a running dive at the gate. He stumbled over the gate and landed in cowdung and was covered from head to foot. Both men were moved on, spending time here and there. They spent time with Seamus McElwaine, with Padraig McKearney, with others.

But not all of the men on the run stayed in the country. Some moved into the cities for a while. Nothing was heard publicly about any of them until May 1984, five months after the Tidey shootout. On Saturday 26 May, gardai and special branch detectives surrounded a house in Dublin's Ballymun estate. Inside, they found Robert 'Goose' Russell. He was arrested and served with an extradition warrant. A further warrant was served in relation to the killing of Prison Officer James Ferris and he was lodged in Portlaoise Prison to await the outcome of the extradition hearings.

But a few months after being caught in Dublin, Robert Russell, feeling that he hadn't much of a chance in beating the extradition rap, was involved in another escape. 24 November was a Sunday. Just before noon, when most of the prisoners and prison staff were attending Mass in E3 wing, twelve IRA men gathered on the landing, Russell among them. Peter Rogers, who still had thirty-six years of a forty-year sentence to complete, produced a gun and held up the staff. All twelve wore fake prison officers' uniforms, covered over with coats. As they passed their first gate to freedom, it accidentally swung shut, and Rogers was trapped with the prison officers. The eleven IRA men discarded their coats and used duplicate keys to get through six further gates. When they came to a steel door they set explosives to blow it open. There was nothing after that except a chainlink fence topped with barbed wire and railings between them and freedom. They blasted the door but it buckled rather than opened. It was jammed shut. They were armed but they surrendered. A couple of hours later a full-scale search of the prison was started and men claimed that they were beaten. A prison officer later confirmed in public that men were beaten in Portlaoise. Robert Russell got three years for the attempted escape.

The legal battles over his extradition continued for years. The Supreme Court handed down its final judgment in the case in January 1988. In a major new departure, they said that Russell was not entitled to exemption from extradition on political grounds, as the methods he used were not those of the government of the day.

Between May and November 1984 nothing more was heard from the remainder of those still at liberty. On a Saturday night, 1 December, the IRA hijacked a van in Pettigo in County Donegal and loaded it up with beer kegs containing explosives. The van was driven across the border towards Beleek and the landmine was placed at the side of the road leading to the Drumrush Lodge Restaurant. A hoax call was made to the RUC about firebombs being at the restaurant and three armed IRA men waited in the darkness for the RUC to respond. Kieran Fleming was part of that IRA unit.

Lance Corporal Alastair Slater had joined the army shortly after his sixteenth birthday in 1973. At Repton Public School he had been interested in mountaineering, venture sports and military drill. He had joined the SAS in 1982. Now on this dark December night he was with an SAS unit, looking for the IRA.

Around 1 am, Tony McBride and another IRA man were in waiting, close to the restaurant, in a van which was to be used to evacuate the IRA unit out of the area. The two in the waiting van spotted what they took to be a car containing civilians up ahead on the road. When the car stopped a man got out. Tony McBride walked towards him. A single shot rang out. McBride had been shot in the leg. The rest of the active service unit could hear his voice. This was followed by a burst of gunfire. A gun battle started. In the darkness twenty-seven year-old Tony McBride and Alastair Slater lay dead. Two other IRA men were wounded. And there was one man missing on the IRA side—Kieran Fleming. An inquest into the death of McBride disclosed that he had ten shots to the back and head. The SAS said he had been unarmed but that he grabbed one of their weapons and they were forced to fire at him. The coroner registered his occupation as a 'Volunteer in the Irish Republican Army'.

Kieran Fleming's body wasn't found for three weeks. He had tried to escape across the Bannagh river which would have left him safely on the other side of the border. He was with another IRA man and sent him across ahead. But he had a fear of water and drowned. At least ten of a fifty-strong search party were arrested by the RUC while they were out looking for him. Kieran Fleming had been active mainly along border areas following his escape. His funeral witnessed very violent scenes with the RUC attempting to remove the tricolour from the coffin and firing plastic bullets at the crowd. One youth suffered a fractured skull and a BBC reporter suffered extensive injuries.

Following that shootout, James Clarke was also arrested on the southern side of the border. He got eighteen years for possession of a weapon. He was also on the attempt to escape from Portlaoise Prison with Robert Russell and got three more years.

Nothing more was heard from the H-Block men until June 1985. On 15 June Mrs Lynn Natividad was the receptionist at the Rubens Hotel in London. It was between 9.30 and 10 pm when she booked in a couple in the names of Mr and Mrs T. Moreton. They paid for the room in advance. She remembered the time afterwards because she had just come back to the desk after watching *Dynasty* on the television. She spent about ten minutes at the desk. She booked the couple into Room 112 which overlooks the Royal Mews.

Peter Sherry was Officer Commanding the East Tyrone

Brigade. In late June he had made a journey to Larne, then took the ferry to Stranraer in Scotland. He travelled to the Central Railway station where he met Patrick Magee. He was tailed by an elite RUC squad, E4A. On this Saturday, 22 June, the two men were followed to 236 Landside Road, Glasgow.

It was 7.40 pm when Detective Inspector Brian Watson went to the door of the groundfloor flat at Number 236. At his back he had seven of the twenty-two officers that had been briefed. Most of them were armed. Watson rapped on the door and Magee opened it. Watson recognised Magee and called on his men to follow him down. Gerry McDonnell was nearby, carrying a Browning automatic in his waistband. He also had a moneybelt with more than £5,000 in it. But more importantly, he was also carrying what the police described as a 'bombing calendar'. Five people in all were arrested at the flat. IRA man McDonnell was also carrying a credit card and birth certificate in the name of Michael Garvey. In the moneybelt were such details as 'London, first floor, 112 front Rubens Hotel, Buckingham Palace Road, BT plus 48'. The following day the police retrieved a bomb in room 112 at the Rubens. It was set for 29 July at 1300 hours. It was booby-trapped and had a 48-day timer attached. The bomb had three to five pounds of explosives, packed in a yellow plastic lunch box behind a bathroom cabinet. It was made up of a nine-volt battery, two 1.5 volt pen batteries, two electronic detonators, the remains of a travel alarm clock, a torch bulb, a mercury tilt switch, a micro switch and pieces of a circuit board. The explosives were wrapped in clingfilm. It was a very sophisticated bomb. Gerry McDonnell was Officer Commanding a unit in England, and they had detailed plans drawn up as to what they were going to do. Gradually, the Seaside Resorts Plot, as it came to be known, unfolded.

It was planned that small bombs would be planted in London, Brighton, Dover, Ramsgate, Southend, Southampton, Blackpool, Eastbourne, Bournemouth, Torquay, Great Yarmouth, Folkstone and Margate between 12 July and 5 August. The effect would be to stretch the security forces, and the presence of IRA marksman Peter Sherry in the vicinity suggested that the IRA would use the bombs as a diversion to get at military targets. The IRA Army Council had received a request from the English unit to launch the bombing campaign, but it would not be drawn on whether or not they had sanctioned it, or even if a decision was made. The Rubens bomb still had six days to run when it was defused.

McDonnell was supposed to have described as an 'oversight' the fact that the Rubens information was written down. He said the IRA always gave warnings and was quoted by the police as saying that if they found a house anywhere in Scotland with explosives in it, it would belong to the IRA, and that it wouldn't be booby-trapped. The police did indeed find such a house.

When Detective Constable Dorrian forced the door of a cellar some distance from the Landside Road flat, a large bag fell on top of him. There were twentiy-five packets of explosives in the cellar, detonators, batteries, booby-trap devices, rifles, ammunition, maps and brochures, timers, alarm clocks, circuit testers and so on. McDonnell was charged with conspiracy to cause explosions.

The IRA said that it was not the intention to harm the Queen by planting the Rubens bomb so close to her home. They did, however, consider that it would be very embarrassing. 'It would be as cutting to her as a bomb,' they said. Gerry McDonnell was sent down for life. Patrick Magee was convicted of the Brighton bombing, in which five Tories had been killed. The bomb had come within a hairsbreadth in 1984 of wiping out the entire British Cabinet.

Nothing more was heard from the escapees between June 1985 and January 1986. The next part of the saga was played out in Holland, at Buitenveldertd, a suburb of Amsterdam. The police came through the windows of the flat throwing flash grenades. It was not normally the type of action the Dutch residents were used to. Having burst through the window the police then politely asked Brendan McFarlane for the keys of the front door. He declined to pass them over. Gerry Kelly was also in the flat. McFarlane had disappeared from the Provos for a while after getting away. His name was linked to the Don Tidey kidnap, and the kidnap of a champion racehorse called Shergar, but there was never any evidence against him on either of these counts. Several miles from the flat the police found a consignment of weapons. The British authorities applied to have the two men extradited back to the North. A long legal wrangle ensued. 'The Hilton' is the nickname given to the prison near Maastricht where McFarlane was held. Its white blocks rise out over the windswept industrial estate which is all around. He was kept in isolation for the next year while the court battles were going on.

The first Dutch court to hear the case disallowed Kelly's extradition, but said that one of McFarlane's offences was not a political one. The judge considered that the two men had used the minimum amount of force when escaping. McFarlane was ordered back to the North and appealed. He said the Bayardo bar was a UVF haunt, and that the UVF had claimed some of the people who had been killed in the attack for which he had been convicted. The Dutch Supreme Court decided to judge the case on the basis of the 1875 Anglo-Dutch Treaty, rather than the more modern 1967 Extradition Act. This was to have significant repercussions, and the two men were ordered back to the North. The Dutch Minister for Justice declined to get an undertaking from the British that the two would be charged with a limited number of offences, and a guarantee in writing that the two should receive no ill treatment as they had in the past.

An appeal to the European Court of Human Rights by Gerry Kelly and Brendan McFarlane was turned down. The Dutch parliament debated the issue. In December 1986 the two men were flown back on board an RAF helicopter. McFarlane was put in the same cell he had slept in the night before the escape, and many of the same warders that had been on when he escaped were in the same positions to welcome him back.

From the time that McFarlane and Kelly were caught in Holland in January, nothing more was heard from any of the escapees until 26 April. Seamus McElwaine had stayed on active service around the border. He had remained a military man, but was developing his own political perspective. McElwaine knew a huge number of people, and moved around County Monaghan in the South, back into Fermanagh in the North, and beyond. He was totally dedicated, spending twenty-four hours a day at being a full-time member of the IRA. On one operation, in which three IRA people took part, one of the Volunteers put his head over a wall afterwards, thinking it was safe to do so. He froze through fear. McElwaine had to grab him and put a gun to his head and told him that he would shoot him if he didn't stay down. He had a gift for recognising people for what they were capable of doing. He could gauge exactly how much anybody was prepared to do. Would they, for example, sell a Republican paper. Or if not, would they even keep a lookout on a window to see what was coming down the road. He operated pretty openly and was well known in the areas he moved. He once gave a speech at a public Sinn Féin meeting in County Fermanagh in the North. He usually planned his own operations, and then spent time narrowing down the risks involved. And he had genuine fear. He was prepared to admit it—which was more than many others were prepared to do.

It was around 5 am on Saturday 26 April 1986. A few days earlier, McElwaine had been with other escapees and had said to one 'Hold on to that until I get back. I'll read it then.' He was referring to a communist newsheet. His friend said that that was no problem, he'd hold on to it for him. Now, McElwaine and Sean Lynch were crossing a field in Mullaghglass, near Roslea in County Fermanagh. Both men were armed. Sean Lynch later told how they headed towards a hole in the hedge to the next field where they had a landmine set.

They stopped just before they went through and listened intently. Everything was okay. Lynch went out through the hole first and McElwaine after him. What they didn't know was that the SAS had found the landmine and had decided to wait. Now, as McElwaine came through, they opened fire. He took three or four steps into the field, hardly realising that he was hit. They ran along parallel with the ditch. Lynch was hit in the leg and chest and several other places.

All that locals heard was a burst of automatic gunfire, followed by a number of single shots some time later. McElwaine was still alive when the SAS soldiers, wearing denims, came up to him and interrogated him. After some time they shot him dead as he lay on the ground. Sean Lynch hid under some bushes nearby and could hear what was going on. The SAS left and regular British soldiers arrived, followed by an RUC divisional Mobile Support Unit. Sean Lynch said afterwards that if it were not for the intervention of the soldiers, he would have been beaten to death by the SAS. It was four hours after the shooting before he was taken by helicopter to Erne Hospital. Carloads of RUC men and women were waiting at the hospital for him. He was later to get twenty-five years. Seamus McElwaine's mother heard on the 10 o'clock news that her son had been shot dead.

Seamus McElwaine had just turned twenty-six. He had been in the IRA for ten years and came from a strong republican background. When he was nineteen he had been Officer Commanding the Fermanagh IRA. In 1981, he had been captured in a house near Roslea. He got life for murder. In 1982 whilst in prison on remand he had stood as a general election candidate in the South and received almost 4,000 votes. The last year of his life was spent always on the run. He was wanted North and South and had little personal money. However, he was popular and had an enormous amount of support from the small landowners of North County Monaghan. His funeral was the biggest in Scotstown for as long as anyone could remember. When the volley of shots were fired over the coffin and into the darkness, there was a deathly silence among the crowd.

It was October 1986 before another escapee was heard from. Jimmy Donnelly had been sentenced two weeks before the escape took place. He was given 208 years, including fifteen for conspiracy to murder, on the word of supergrass Christopher Black. He was caught on the way out of the jail. When he was waiting to appear on escape charges the entire case against him collapsed when the appeal court refused to uphold the convictions on the word of Black alone. He managed to get bail in October, never showed for his trial and is still on the run.

On 19 December Patrick McIntyre, who had been caught shortly after the escape, managed to get rehabilitation parole. This parole was offered to prisoners near the end of their sentences as a carrot for good behaviour.

The Provos didn't like it, as it was applied arbitrarily, and could be used to cause division. It had taken McIntyre nine years to get freedom. He had lost it on Easter Sunday morning in 1978. He was one of seven Provos that crossed the border from Donegal to Derry that day. They were supposed to lead the Easter parade through the Bogside and Creggan at which the Vice-President of Sinn Féin, Daithi O'Conaill, delivered the oration. When it was all over the Provos made their way to the Rossville Street flats, took off their gear and glasses and started their journey back. They had been told that the road was clear but they were arrested by a joint British Army/RUC patrol. The entire episode had been closely monitored from a helicopter overlooking the scene.

Patrick McIntyre was the fifth of a family of nine and his

father edited the *Donegal People's Press*. He did his Leaving Certificate in 1976, and then a six-month AnCO course. He worked on a building site in Letterkenny for a while and then quit. While at school he had given little indication to his friends that he was inclined towards the Provos. But in 1978 he wound up in RUC custody. He signed an incriminating statement about the attempted murder of a UDR man in late 1977 near Castlederg in County Tyrone, spent eighteen months on remand and refused to recognise the court. When he appeared, he got fifteen years. James Clarke, who was up on the same charge, and who escaped at the same time, got eighteen years. But when McIntyre got parole, and didn't turn up, the RUC and the gardai went looking for him.

In the townland of Cashlings, between Killybegs and Killgar, the gardai raided what they considered to be a safe house shortly after 8 am on 6 January 1987. When armed detectives moved into the house they found a man wearing nothing but underpants lying in a bed. They woke him up. He said he was Colm McGuire and refused to answer any more questions. They arrested him on suspicion of being a member of the IRA. It took an hour for the gardai to take their prisoner to Ballyshannon. A solicitor was sent for. Following a consultation the solicitor mentioned to the gardai that they had Patrick McIntyre in custody. The gardai immediately said that they wanted to talk to him about a robbery in Ballyshannon just before Christmas, and so they started to question him about this robbery.

On 7 January, when an extradition hearing was due to take place in front of District Justice McMenamin at Ballyshannon, about 100 Sinn Féin people turned up to support McIntyre. An RUC man called Robert Herron slipped past the crowd to identify McIntyre as an escaper. Herron was allowed to leave the court but the gardai insisted that the doors would have to remain closed for some time after that. This meant that the demonstrators had no idea who Herron was.

Superintendent Murphy had signed the extension order, as allowed under the Offences Against the State Act 1939. The extension order allows the gardai to detain a person for a 24-hour period, following an initial 24-hour period, if they are of the belief that this detention is necessary for the investigation of crime. But what was in the mind of the officer signing this extension order is relevant to the validity of the order. In the event, McIntyre was ordered to be extradited. He went into the High Court looking for a reversal of that decision.

On 3 April the Supreme Court in Dublin ruled, in another case, that when a detention order is signed there must be evidence proffered as to why the order was signed. There was no such evidence in McIntyre's case and so he was freed. There was consternation among the gardai as he was about to leave the court. The prison officer refused to let McIntyre go, even though he had been ordered free by the court. There were further legal arguments as to whether McIntyre could be served with another nineteen extradition warrants on the spot. The judge said he was free to go. Yet he was still handcuffed. Patrick McIntyre became very agitated; he didn't think he was going to get away. Finally, he was released.

McIntyre ran from the court, and jumped onto the back of a waiting motorbike and was soon lost in the rushing traffic along Dublin's quays. The gardai still have nineteen warrants for his extradition. He is still on the run and free at the time of writing.

On Thursday, 2 April, 1987, there was a knock on the door of a small house in Ardoyne. Papillon was at home. His real name was Larry Marley. He had been released almost a year earlier. Kathleen Marley was carrying their two-week-old son Setanta as he opened the living-room door, leading to the small porch. 'Who's there?' she asked.

A male voice responded, giving the name of a well-known person in the area. As Larry Marley moved to open the door he glanced through a small pane of glass at the top of the door. Quickly he moved back towards the living-room. A shotgun blast rang out and the glass was shattered from the outside. Splinters flew into the ceiling. Larry turned and motioned to Kathleen to get down, and then a gunman fired at least ten rounds from a Browning automatic pistol through the door. Larry Marley was hit in the chest several times. Kathleen and Setanta were covered in glass and wood. Larry was taken to the Mater Hospital but was dead ninety minutes later. At the time of his killing by loyalist assassins, the small Ardoyne district was saturated with RUC and British Army patrols. All the exits were covered—with the exception of the one the gunmen used.

The following morning, when members of the family travelled to the morgue to identify his body, they were stopped and questioned by RUC patrols, and later that same evening the RUC took up battle positions near the Marley home, as friends and neighbours called to pay their respects. Over that weekend the RUC maintained their positions, and on the Monday the family made their first attempt to bury Larry Marley.

All the roads leading out of Ardoyne were blocked, and vehicles belonging to mourners were stopped and searched. Shortly before 10 am, the tricolour-draped coffin was carried out of the house. The RUC attempted to move in on the coffin and fighting started between the police and mourners. The coffin was carried back inside. Larry Marley's funeral had become a flashpoint in the long-running battle with the RUC over funerals. Republican dead were rarely buried in peace. But very little had prepared anyone for what was to happen over the next few days. A priest, Fr Pat Fitzgerald, talked with the RUC, and told them that there would be nothing on the coffin except the tricolour—there would be no cap and gloves. He asked them to move back. The RUC refused. And for the next three hours there were skirmishes with the RUC. Just before dinner time Larry Marley junior told the mourners that the funeral was postponed. He asked everyone to come back the following day. He asked the Catholic Cardinal, Tomás O'Fiaich, to intercede with the Secretary of State, Tom King.

The RUC said they were trying to stop any paramilitary display. The IRA had honoured Marley on the previous Saturday night at the Republican Memorial in Ardoyne when three armed and masked men had fired the volley. On that Monday another priest, Fr Gerry Reynolds, and a Methodist minister had talked to the RUC and Sinn Féin.

There was a large demonstration that night, and on the Tuesday the coffin was brought out again. The RUC presence was doubled from the previous day, and again the RUC moved forward towards the coffin. Other RUC units started to move in from beyond the crowd. In scenes reminiscent of South Africa vicious hand-to-hand fighting broke out between the crowd and the police. Television viewers were treated to the sight of a coffin dancing on the shoulders of the bearers as the RUC moved about, batoning people. The coffin was brought back into the house and mourners and the RUC fought on the small streets of Ardoyne. Larry Marley was as much trouble in death as he had ever been in life.

Sinn Féin representative Martin McGuinness addressed the crowd from a bedroom window in the Marley home. Over 1,000 people listened as he said: 'We are not proceeding with this funeral under these circumstances. . . . It looks as if we are going to have to make a stand on this issue otherwise someone is going to be killed at one of these funerals.' There was more confrontation with the RUC. People leaving the area were not allowed back in. Larry Marley junior again announced that the funeral would be postponed for another twenty-four hours. 3,000 people marched through Ardoyne in protest at the behaviour of the police.

Shortly before 10 am on the Wednesday, the coffin came through the door for the third time. The destination was the Holy Cross Chapel where Requiem Mass was due to be said prior to the actual burial. It took seven hours of sporadic fighting, bitter arguments with the police and fierce resistance to bury him.

On the 45-minute walk to the chapel, there were several violent clashes. And following the Mass, rows and rows of mourners linked arms and stopped the RUC gaining access to the coffin. The cortege paused briefly as they passed the Marley home, and made its way down Oldpark Road. Dozens of black taxis, driven two abreast down the road, ferried the mourners to the graveyard. An emotional oration was delivered by Martin McGuinness. He asked everybody to look around and stare at the RUC, in silence. 'They have just looked defeat in the face,' McGuinness said, 'we are going to win.' The *Guardian* referred to the funeral as the 'biggest display of republican support since the hunger strikes.'

When the funeral passed through Falls Road, old women shook their fists at the soldiers who led the columns of thirty-five landrovers. Patients at the Royal Victoria Hospital came out in dressing-gowns and slippers to pay their last respects. The *Belfast Telegraph* said, 'the world must have got the impression of a police state, quite unjustified, where men in riot helmets were dictating how a man should be buried.' American network CBS called the BBC Belfast office and asked 'why don't they let them bury this poor guy?' Throughout the entire episode, Kathleen Marley had taken the brunt of the assault. It was the family who took the decision to defy the conditions under which the police wanted him buried. She could be heard crying as the coffin danced in the air outside the house, surrounded by 300 RUC men. There had been suggestions that Sinn Féin were somehow manipulating the funeral to cause confrontation with the RUC. She called a press conference to refute those claims.

Kathleen and Larry shared the same birth date. Through all the years, she had waited for him, while he was in jail, planning escapes. When the H-Block escape took place, Brendan McFarlane was credited with leading it and Larry Marley said nothing, just laughed to himself. It was a standing joke among those who knew him that he would resent having to leave the prison by the front door, having planned so many escapes throughout the years since the early seventies. His funeral turned out to be one of the most violent for years.

Padraig McKearney had gone on to put into practice what he had been talking about under the floorboards. He had talked about 'the third phase of the struggle' and 'holding isolated pockets of resistance'. This involved attacking isolated RUC barracks right across the North. Between January 1984 and the end of 1986, more than seventy such attacks had taken place. More than thirty-five RUC men had been killed and more than sixty wounded. Mortars were used in many of the attacks, but by and large, they followed a pattern. The Ballygawley attack in County Tyrone, was typical.

Saturday evening, 7 December 1985, found McKearney outside Ballygawley barracks. Heavily armed units of the East Tyrone IRA surrounded the barracks. (Patrick Kelly had taken over as Officer Commanding after Peter Sherry was arrested in Scotland.) When the IRA were in position, one man moved forward towards the gate. Just before 7 pm two RUC men moved towards the gate from the inside; it was time for a shift change. When they opened the gate, the IRA man stepped forward and shot both men dead at point-blank range, and took their weapons. The rest of the IRA unit moved into the barracks, carrying armalites and AK-47s, and raked the front of the building with gunfire. They fired on three RUC men running out of the back. They then demolished the barracks with a bomb.

On Friday 8 May 1987 the IRA took a blue Toyota van from a business in Dungannon, County Tyrone. Around 6 pm that same evening, a mechanical digger was taken from a farm at Lissassley Road, also near Dungannon. IRA men stayed at the farm while the rest drove away with the digger and van. They headed towards Loughgall, a small village not far away.

On the approach to the quiet village the road sweeps up to the brow of a hill. There are no more than 350 people living there. There is a slight bend on the road, and then the RUC station appears on the right-hand side. The station, which stood on its own, was manned on a part-time basis only, for two hours in the morning, and between 5 and 7 pm. There were four small cottages nearby. A small bit further down the road, twelve schoolgirls had arrived early to the church hall for a Girls Friendly Society meeting. Eight IRA men, dressed in blue boiler suits, gloves and runners, prepared to carry out the IRA's twenty-second attack of the year on an RUC barracks. What they didn't know was that there had been intense security in the village earlier in the week, and that the RUC men who normally worked in the barracks had been removed. They drove into the village with a 200lb bomb in the front bucket of the digger at 7.17 pm. There were three IRA men on the digger and five in the van.

As the digger drew level with the station it swung in and smashed through the perimeter fence. The front was jammed up against the building. The bomb was primed and men started to run back towards the van. But it was already too late. The SAS and RUC had by now surrounded the IRA. While the IRA unit had concentrated on the station, they had closed in from both sides. They opened up. Within a couple of minutes, the eight IRA men, including Padraig McKearney, lay dead. Eye-witnesses said that some of them were shot trying to get away. The ambush also claimed the life of Anthony Hughes, and his brother Oliver was also injured badly. Both had been wearing boiler suits, and had come into Loughgall looking for a machine part. One local women, Mrs Beggs, had a lucky escape when bullets came through her window. Police video crews took film footage of the killings.

Within two minutes the entire area was saturated with roadblocks and hundreds of RUC and British Army moved into the area. As the light faded helicopters with searchlights fanned the surrounding fields, apparently looking for anybody who might have escaped. A .357 Luger Magnum was recovered at the scene from the body of one IRA man. It had been taken from Constable William Clements when he was shot dead at

Ballygawley, eighteen months earlier. The revolver had been used in three separate killings since that point, and one attempted killing. It was not clear whether any of the eight IRA men managed to return fire. It was 4 am the following morning before RUC convoys started to take the bodies up the back road to Portadown morgue. The Irish government said that it was the fault of the IRA men themselves that they had been killed.

In November 1987, several events outside the control of the escapees still on the run occurred. Dublin dentist John O'Grady was kidnapped and was finally released following various confrontations with the gardai in the South. It then emerged that O'Grady had been brutalised during his captivity, a new development in Ireland. His kidnapper was involved on the fringes of the Irish National Liberation Army. In 1987 that organisation had killed at least fourteen of its own members in a bitter internal feud. Around the same time that O'Grady was freed, the *Eksund* was captured off the French coast. She was carrying hundreds of weapons, and the word went out that these were destined for the IRA.

Then on Remembrance Sunday, eleven Protestants were killed by an IRA bomb in Enniskillen. These three events prompted the Irish government to start a major nationwide search for other alleged shipments of arms which were rumoured to have reached the IRA.

In November and December, more than 70,000 homes were searched. Very little was actually found. On 1 November, Paul Kane and Dermot Finucane were caught near Granard in County Longford.

Kane had been caught shortly after the escape, but when his conviction on the word of Black collapsed, he managed to get bail on the escape charges. He jumped bail and went on the run. He was arrested in Granard under Section 30 of the Offences Against the State Act and held for 48 hours. The following was related to the High Court in Dublin when Kane took an action challenging the legal basis of his arrest and detention.

The gardai had no legal power to hold Kane without charge after the 48 hours were up. But towards the end of that period, it became known that the RUC were 'interested' in him. He was let go at 1.25 pm on 3 November. The gardai had discovered, as a result of the McIntyre case, that they could not arrest and detain under the Offences Against the State Act in order to execute an extradition warrant. Upon his release, he was followed through Granard by teams of detectives who said they were monitoring his movements to see whom he would associate with. They said they believed that Kane would lead them to other people. This monitoring was overt, they just walked behind him through the streets.

Paul Kane managed to hitch a lift from a BBC crew and got as far as Cavan town, where he contacted a local solicitor. The teams of detectives who followed him were to claim afterwards that none of them knew that he was an escaper. They stuck to this even though this fact had been in most of the papers the previous day. Kane was free to move anywhere he wished. The gardai stuck to their story that they did not wish to talk to him, or that they knew he was wanted in the North. Then a prison officer was brought to the solicitor's office and positively identified Kane as an escaper.

As darkness began to fall the gardai followed Kane with a searchlight. They were afterwards to claim that they were still looking for clues as to who Kane's associates might be. They wanted to talk to his associates. He was being followed by at least a dozen gardai. Kane jumped into a car. Garda cars and Kane's car jostled on the narrow country roads, until finally the Bluebird that Kane was in came to a halt and Kane dived through a hedge. A garda ran after him, even though he was later to say the only reason he was following him was to observe what was going on; the garda dived after Kane 'to keep him under observation'. There was a drop into briars and mud. It was dark. There was some sort of a struggle, and Kane was arrested for breach of the peace by assault. He was charged also with damage to a garda's watch and even though there was never any watch produced it was classified as malicious damage and enough to hold Kane. He got bail on these minor charges the following day but then a provisional extradition warrant was served on him.

The High Court, in an action taken by Kane, held that the garda surveillance of Kane was not effectively moving detention. Motor bikes, and flashing cars, and jeeps of armed men screeched their way through Dublin's streets, bringing Kane from one court to another.

At the time of writing both Kane and Finucane intend

fighting the extradition. It is a long and costly process and can sometimes take years. Tony Kelly and Seamus Clarke were also caught during those raids. They were taken in a house in Kilbarrack in Dublin. Kelly got seven years in January 1988. He had been up previously on a possession charge in the South in 1985 and had skipped.

The following people are still free: Kevin Barry Artt, Paul Brennan, Seamus Campbell, Jimmy Donnelly, John Fryers, Terence Kirby, Anthony McAllister, Patrick McIntyre, Dermot McNally and J.J. Smith. Eight of the original nineteen were never caught, one got bail on the escape charges and one got rehabilitation parole. Three were killed, and the rest were caught. Those who were caught in the immediate aftermath of the trial faced charges of escaping and the murder of Prison Officer James Ferris.

13

Men on the Run

In the course of researching the escape it was necessary to interview dozens of people, some supporters, and others who were peripherally involved in the escape. Many of those who had intimate involvement with planning and executing the escape were not actually on it. Chief among these, as we have seen, was Papillon, or Larry Marley, assassinated by loyalists in early 1987. Many of those who were involved in planning the escape were released in the following years, but were reluctant to be named because conspiracy charges could still be laid against them. But it was also necessary to talk to escapees themselves.

Interviews with the escapees took weeks to set up. They were carried out in different locations, and at different times, in the South. All had returned to active service with the IRA and were on the run at the time of interview. They could not see any other way around the military encounter with the British Army, the RUC and the UDR. All of them were prepared to see it through. All know that their options at the moment, if they don't get caught or killed, are very limited. They will always be on the run, even if they leave the IRA.

The first escaper was interviewed over a period of three days. He was part of the group that had spent a week under floorboards following the escape. He had an important role during the escape, in taking a Wing, and had known about the plans for weeks before. For two months prior to the interview he had been unable to move around the country at will. And during the three days, he would only venture out at night to local places. He had been debriefed by the IRA immediately after his escape, and then put on freeze. For months, he had taken no part in anything. He took time out to reach a mental and physical peak. As he described what life on the run was like he paced the room back and forth, throwing his arms wide to express a point, cracking jokes and laughing a lot.

He always has to keep moving, sometimes he might be no more than two nights in a house. He's lucky if he gets a week in one place. And all the time, he has to watch his back and take care of his own security. 'I try to live as normal a life as possible. You need that to stay sane, to take the pressure. There is always the knowledge that you could be shot dead or arrested in an hour's time and it's very important to have the right attitude. You have to adjust to that situation. There are certain things you can and cannot do.'

He takes different names in different places. In most of the houses he stays, North and South, people don't even ask what his name is. They have no idea that he is a Long Kesh escaper, or that he is active with the IRA. In the house where the interview took place the householder was not aware of who he was. 'People just want to keep us, to do their bit. They feel as if they're doing something. I never talk about where I've come from, or where I'm going, or my family life or private life or social life.' Social life can be constricted when there are raids happening, or there is a security clampdown. For months on end it may be necessary to stay in one location never moving out.

Over the years he has slept in beds, under beds, in haysheds, in cars, in forests, in attics, in wardrobes, in hedges and bolt-holes. At one point he lived with Padraig McKearney for three weeks in hedges close to the border. There was a security clampdown at the time and they couldn't move. They were close to an old shed which leaked a lot. The water dripped on both of them constantly. They were armed with AK-47s, Magnum pistols and a grenade each and were dressed in combat uniforms. After the three weeks, he thought he was going to die, that he had pneumonia; he had a chest infection and spent two weeks in bed.

On active service nearly all movement across country means carrying a sleeping bag on your shoulder. Chocolate bars and lumps of cheese are the mainstay diet. It would be days or weeks before the operation is over. Sometimes he might arrive at a border house late at night. The kids might be woken up to act as lookout while he recuperates. 'Some of them are kept off school to keep watch for us. . . . The people who give us safe houses are not necessarily republican. Some of them are in Fianna Fáil, some

152

in Fine Gael, some in the SDLP and some even in the Progressive Democrats! They are houses that never come under suspicion, and are not likely to be.'

During the November 1987 raids in the South all IRA people on the run had to stay put. There was a total freeze on movement. At one point during that period he stayed in a garda house.

There was one 'near thing' when he was moving. He was in the boot of a car with another IRA man. The area they were leaving was in the process of being surrounded by gardai and army. There was a leak in the exhaust pipe of the car and fumes were entering the boot. They banged to get out. They had sore heads and were very sick for days afterwards.

'I have been stopped at checkpoints by gardai, and British Army and RUC. I gave identification in most cases and was just waved on.' The identification was false. The escaper is not recognisable from any of the old photographs which are available. The only thing that goes against him in the South is his Northern accent. 'It's a dead giveaway. Some of us have taken elocution lessons to try and tone it down.'

Between houses he may have to walk up to ten miles. If he goes by car he never drives. There are full-time drivers whose only job is to ferry IRA people around. The only circumstances under which he may drive a car is if it has been hijacked. He has stayed in Protestant houses, North and South. In the North, there are houses belonging to teachers, civil servants and managers that are open to the IRA. 'We have our own hairdressers and we use different hairstyles and clothes for different areas. One day you might be wearing a three-piece suit and walking down Grafton Street. The next day you could be wearing wellingtons with hay in them and a cap pulled over your eyes in the country.' Different towns have different styles of clothing. 'In the country people tend to wear darker clothes than in the towns and cities.'

There are certain rules, an unwritten code, which they adhere to in safe houses. They do not get personally involved with women in the house. 'Whatever about going out for a night with an unattached woman, it would be detrimental to get involved with a married woman.' Word would very quickly get around and that house would be lost. Personal relationships are very difficult. There can never be a normal life. There are disappearances for weeks on end. There is never any guarantee that he will live beyond the next hour.

Many of the escapees have indeed found personal relationships very difficult. Many have resigned themselves to the fact that they can never find a home life, and some have divorced to allow their former wives to try and find some normal life. The children of those former relationships are unlikely to see their father, except perhaps once or twice a year, in covert circumstances, south of the border.

Laid up in houses for long periods he read a lot. In the couple of weeks prior to the interview, he has read *Ireland in Crisis* by Raymond Crotty, *Error of Judgement* by Chris Mullin, *Against the Tide* by Noel Browne, *Inside an English Jail* by Raymond McLaughlin and *Goodnight Sisters* ... by Nell McCafferty. He keeps a library of books in one location, picking them up along the way and sending them on. But discussing politics is a constant topic—where the IRA is going, where Sinn Féin is going, what all the other political parties are doing and why. He watches and listens to all news broadcasts, North and South, and all current affairs and political programmes. He maintains an ongoing interest in all public personalities and people in the media. 'If someone says something about us I try and find out what their political background is and what their vested interests are.' This means that reporters' political backgrounds are scrutinised, whether they are Workers Party, for example, or Fianna Fáil, or Labour, and what they say is judged accordingly.

In the safe houses there is almost inevitably intense political debate. He is a selfavowed socialist, and always makes a point of talking to the children, politicising them. Sometimes there might be one of the children attending university. He will argue with the version of history being taught, and argue passionately that the education system is part of the establishment and its only aim is to 'preserve the State'. 'Our socialist politics contradict all of that. Sometimes there's trouble. Maybe there's only one republican in the house, maybe a father or a daughter. And the parents get frightened. They think their kids will go off and join the IRA.'

He takes the view that selling *An Phoblacht / Republican News*, the official publication of the republican movement, is every bit as important as carrying out assaults on RUC stations with AK-

47s. He has involved himself deeply in the changing politics of the Provos, drawing up discussion papers, submitting ideas of how things can be changed.

'We don't want to be treated as heroes where we stay. There is no such thing as an officer class in the IRA. We are all Volunteers. We rely totally on other people for everything. We are the fish in the sea and without these people we don't survive.' All clothes are gifts. Tobacco and newspapers and food and shelter are all supplied. He gets a subsidy of £10 a week as a Volunteer in the IRA. Married men get £20. If he runs into debt the IRA will clear that debt. But they don't need that much money. 'The only problem comes when it's our turn to buy a round of drink when we're out!' If one gets some money from a relative, and there are a bunch of IRA people together, it is divided equally amongst the rest. Sometimes they 'save' the weekly tenner for a break. On a weekend off politics is not discussed, the IRA is not discussed; a break is a break.

Life can be very varied. One week he might be drawing up posters for a meeting, the next moving weapons and explosives towards the border and across the border. If there is trouble in an area, such as the discovery of arms and ammunition, he would be involved in trying to find out what went wrong, and straightening of units in a particular area. Since the escape, he has been involved in restructuring the IRA, North and South. 'You can thank the escapees for that.' The entire Army has been on 'internment standby' for the last year, so that the introduction of internment would not result in the activists getting picked up. He is also involved in internal enquiries and courts martial. He is also involved in other IRA departments—Intelligence, Training, Overseas. He could be asked to go overseas tomorrow and would have to know what was involved. There is a constant input of information and ideas from the escapees into all the various departments. They have changed the face of the IRA.

'People within the IRA come up to us and say "What are you doing at the moment? Are you doing anything?" As if we were doing nothing except sitting around all day. Jesus Christ! We never stop working.' He uses his initiative a lot, in suggesting different operations that could be carried out. He would not suggest anything he would not do himself. 'One day you're talking to a journalist and the next day you're sitting on a landmine.' He has managed to build up a 'clean network' of safe houses and contacts. This means that he can operate outside the traditional republican network. That these networks are 'clean' had already been borne out by the fact that he has not been caught to date. During the November 1987 raids, there were more that fifty people the gardai could have arrested if they had found them. Only four wanted people were caught. 'If I make one new contact, I could get ten safe houses out of that.'

If he is in a safe house, and the government increases taxes, 'or something crazy like that', people are annoyed and disgruntled. 'We get a few more houses and we build up a small bit more as a result.' When eleven people were killed at Enniskillen on Remembrance Sunday, he was shattered. It was wrong. 'I felt sorry for the victims, and their families, and the unit that had done it.' But all support didn't disappear for the IRA as a result. In some areas, people who had never supported the IRA did so. 'We lost one house out of 200 as a result of Enniskillen.'

Following the interview, he travelled southwards, towards Cork. Over the three days, he had gone out each night to local bars. It had been months since he had been able to do that. Sometimes, he appeared slightly reckless about his own security. On several occasions, he bumped into gardai but was not recognised.

With another escaper, it was possible to meet him only at night. For two nights in a row, the escaper came across the fields after dark, and stayed until late, moving out from the house before dawn. Garda checks in the area were constant. This was the same man who had got caught up unknowingly in the Tidey kidnap in Leitrim and was almost caught. As with the other escapees the photographs available bear little resemblance to what he looks like today. He was very nervous about speaking to journalists. He had known about the escape a few weeks before-hand. Just after the warders opened the doors of the cells that Sunday afternoon he had armed himself with the blade of a plane. 'I can't remember all of this. It was over four years ago. All I heard was "move". There was no one near the button I was watching. The screw had gone to the toilet. I stayed between the grilles on the wings controlling movement.'

The warders were completely bewildered by what had happened. 'They hadn't a clue what was going on. It was great having control of the Block, having them under our control for a change, even if it was only for a while.' He got into the lorry when it arrived and was told that there was to be no talking. 'We couldn't see anything much out of the lorry. I was right in front, at the shutters, and you could see the fellah in front of you but that was it. I remember at the Tally Lodge, when everything went wrong, the OC came up and said "right lads, the ball's busted". I remember those words. They're the ones he used—"the ball's busted".' He managed to get away across the fields and on to the road, but had no idea where he was going. 'There was a car and a pile of boys already in it and me and a load of others trying to get in as well. The car took off with me hanging out one window.' They then hijacked another car, and he eventually ended up under the floorboards.

'Of the eight men that were under those floorboards, two were killed and four were caught. I was with all of them from time to time in different houses. We were in two groups of four under the boards. One group of four would be passed the grub, and I remember we'd have to crawl up and get it. I hit the beam when I was trying to get a comfortable position. I could hear the lads whispering up "who hit that beam?" It was dark. Nobody knew who did it, until now'. It took four weeks before he was taken across the border.

He was from Belfast originally, and he imagined that once he was across the border, everything would be all right. 'Nothing had prepared us for life on the run. We still had no grasp of what being on the run in the South actually meant. One guy thought we could just walk about. He wanted to get out. He couldn't take it. We knew nothing about the South.' He could only venture out at night in the beginning. And most movement was through the fields. 'I hadn't seen a field before in my life. We had to get used to ditches and drains and all of that. And then when were starting to get settled in, along came Don Tidey.'

None of the escapees are armed at any time. His life has been more settled in that he has stayed in one area for most of the time. At times it is possible to socialise without attracting attention. More often than not this is not possible.

At different times he lived with Kieran Fleming, Padraig McKearney and Seamus McElwaine. He was very much affected by each of the three deaths, and even talking about the men, years later, he is still visibly shaken. He has adjusted well to living in the country and is known by another name to most people. He is still as committed as ever to the IRA, but the constant strain of being on the run has its price and can take its toll. Again, personal relationships on any long-term basis are very difficult. And while socialising, 'letting go' can present a problem. In some cases you have to let go and care a little less about safety in order to hold on to it, and to hold on to sanity, and to some degree of normality. All of the escapees strive towards normality in their lives in so far as is possible. But their lives are far from normal.

The next escaper found out about the escape the day before it was due to take place. 'I knew what was going down on that Sunday morning, but we weren't supposed to discuss it with anyone. I couldn't take the escape in. I never went to Mass, but I went that morning. There was a buzz there. We were in lock-up after that and then let out. One of the lads came over to me and said "there's a hood under your pillow". As soon as the screw got as far as the gate we got the word to go.'

When John Adams was shot, there was some panic—'that wasn't in the plan'—and then the long wait for the lorry which arrived late that day. 'I remember the grub had to be unloaded. I think it was boiled eggs and lettuce and onions and bread. The people in the Circle unloaded the lorry and took the grub onto the Wings. We were told to sit tight, that we would be given the word.' Then there was another wait while final preparations were made.

'When we were in the lorry, I couldn't imagine what it was like to be getting out. We were all very nervous.' He was one of six people who got into a warder's car. 'The gate had been open. We could see it. And it started to close. Someone shouted "go through it". The car was turning and swerving. We tried to crash through and it busted open. My head was jammed under the back seat. We were in a two-door car and I got out the side window. All the screws were shouting and a Brit at the gate fired his weapon. I thought I was going to be shot.' He wasn't .

Originally from Belfast he felt he was 'under a lot of pressure' to go back there. He asked to be allowed back but was turned down. At one point shortly afterwards, he was in the same house for six months in the South. The Belfast Brigade ordered him to stay in the South. 'I wanted to go back as a Volunteer. I was cheesed off. I spent six months just sitting tight.... When you are doing something it occupies your mind. Most of the time you just sit around waiting. If I was in Belfast I know I'd get caught. But sometimes I think that two months in Belfast and then getting caught would be better than here.'

The long periods of being indoors, waiting, can also take its toll. 'Once me and another escaper were in for months, and then we went out for a pint. We had two drinks and got sick, we couldn't take it. We weren't used to it. We just played scrabble a lot. Then he moved away, and another escaper arrived, and we played scrabble a lot. I read a lot of books and listen to tapes—blues, and traditional, and classical as well. It's really boring. It sounds really shit, but that's it.'

During the November 1987 raids he also had to 'sit tight'. 'It was hard to move around. I was driven here and there in cars. If I was lucky I managed to get a bus ride.' He 'occasionally' gets to see his family when they come to visit him in the South. Two weeks before this interview took place, he saw his sister for a few hours. There had been a gap of two months before that, when he hadn't see any members of his family. The thing that bothers him most is just 'sitting around'.

During that November, he stayed in watching television and listening to the news, trying to figure out where the searches were concentrating. 'We had to sit tight and hope the house was safe, and it was. We stayed there until a couple of days before Christmas. We got moved again, and got out for an hour on Christmas Eve. We were moved here last week, and I'm moving again now. We slept during the day and stayed awake at night, watching. We had no guns. When you're on active service, you're always relying on other people.'

He isn't sure about his future. He knows that the options are limited. 'I have some hope, but you're not in control of the future. If we were told that there was some hope, then we'd go for it. I would like to see my family in Belfast. I'm on edge up here. You're always being watched and you have to watch out in case you get into trouble. In Belfast, I'm not inhibited. It's not a parochial thing with me. At least not any more. If I was to ever settle down at all, it would be in the country. You have far more privacy.' He had no more than a few hours to be interviewed, and then he was on the move towards the border as soon as morning came.

Another escaper has his hair dyed, and again, looks completely different than the available photographs would suggest.

He is cautious and while he has 'no problems' giving an interview about the escape he does not want to name others. The main problem, as with all the escapees, is that they are fearful that conspiracy charges could be laid against them if they are ever caught.

The escape plan was gone over again that Sunday morning. 'Nobody wanted to be the one to fuck it up.' He was in the same cell as another escaper yet neither knew that the other was on the escape. When the plan went wrong at the Tally Lodge he was one of the first across the wire. He ripped his hand, but didn't notice it at the time. Gerry Kelly landed beside him, and both men asked each other if they were all right. They watched as Kieran Fleming 'ploughed his way through' the wire after getting tangled up. He managed to get into the car Padraig McKearney was driving. Then they took another car with a sunroof, 'Me and another fellah had our heads out driving down the road. That's when I found out that my hand was cut fairly deeply. There were eight of us in the car.' They got another car, and split into two groups of four. He managed to get away.

His life has been pretty much like the rest of those on the run, one of constant vigilance. On one occasion, while the interview was being conducted in a bar, two people appeared to display an unnecessary interest in him. Within minutes, the people who were backing him up checked out the two. It took twenty minutes. By then, it was known who they were, where they lived, where they worked, and what their politics were. As it turned out, there was nothing to be worried about. He was more on edge than most of the escapees. Different men handle being on the run in different ways. Some will push their luck to the limit. Others are very cautious. And some, while not actually enjoying being on the run, have managed to develop and thrive under very adverse circumstances.

When they escaped from Long Kesh in September 1983, none could have guessed what lay ahead: that three would die at the hands of the SAS; that many more would get caught in Holland, Scotland, Ireland; but most of all, they had simply not been prepared for the undercover life they would have to lead. Again and again, it came across in the course of the interview that some of the men thought that they would be able to walk about freely. They knew little or nothing about life in the South. It has taken them years to learn. Some have settled into the life. It is

160

debatable whether some of them will ever accept their situation.

What each and every one of them recognises is that their options for the future are limited. If they stay on active service, they may be caught or killed. They may be lucky and evade death and capture. If they decide that they have had enough, and settle down, there are still risks. What differentiates the Long Kesh '83 escapees is that they will always be on the run. Because they know that if they are caught anywhere, they will be returned to the North. They will serve long sentences. This, more than anything else, means that there can be no going back. Ever.

14

Men in Jail

Gerry Kelly, one of the two escapees caught in Holland, was sent to Crumlin Road Jail in Belfast. The remainder of the prisoners were in the Blocks. In order to visit him at the prison, you have to go through innumerable gates.

Firstly a visitor's pass has to be sent out by Kelly. This pass is produced at the jail itself and then you wait in a room until you get called. All possessions with the exception of cigarettes are taken away. Money is sealed in an envelope and you are not allowed to open the envelope within the confines of the prison.

Gerry Kelly looks fit and healthy as he awaits the verdict of the court on the charge of attempted murder of John Adams. A prison officer sits close for the entire duration of the half-hour visit. His life has been full of escape attempts. He was married and has a fourteen-year-old son but now he is divorced.

He was from a family of eleven children and worked in Belfast Corporation Electricity Department. He joined the Fianna — the junior wing of the IRA—in 1971 and was arrested for a robbery in County Louth. He got two years, a stiff sentence in those early days, and imagined that his life as a teenager was over.

He escaped from St Pat's Detention Centre in Dublin by going through the nearby women's prison. He joined the IRA and remained active and on the run until March 1973. He was part of an IRA unit that planted bombs at the Old Bailey and New Scotland Yard in London. The plan was that the entire IRA unit would be back in Dublin by the time the bombs went off.

He noticed the plain-clothes policemen around Heathrow airport as they prepared to board the plane. The eight people were returning to Ireland in twos. Paul Holmes was with him. Holmes was asked to accompany the police out of the departure lounge and Gerry Kelly thought 'poor Paul'. Travelling as Mr Lyons, Kelly was asked to leave the plane as the captain wanted to speak to him. Dressed in a suit and a yellow shirt, he asked 'what's going on?' He kept the charade up for as long as he could.

He was given two twenty-year sentences and went on a hunger strike to be repatriated back to the North. He refused to eat and kept up his fast for more than 60 days. The Price sisters, sentenced for similiar offences, continued their fast for more than 200 days and were force fed. Four of the eight were sent back to the North to serve out their sentences eventually.

While in England, Kelly had tried to escape from Wormwood Scrubs but was caught as he clambered over the last wall. He tried to get away again from the Lagan Valley Hospital in the North, and from Cage 11 Long Kesh. In Musgrave Park Hospital in 1982, he was using a bolt cutters and a screw driver to cut through the last wire fence when he was spotted by a nurse. She called the police.

He laughs about the escape attempts. He had 'developed a slightly pessimistic attitude about escapes'. He remembers the night before he left for London to carry out the bombings which landed him in jail, he watched *The Glass House*.

The film was about a jail experience in the United States. The night before the escape in September 1983, he watched *Escape from Devil's Island* on the video in the canteen. He considered that this was a good omen for a change. McFarlane and Kelly were standing at the back of the canteen and Kelly rubbed his hands together and he was sure it was going to work.

The events at the wire at the Tally Lodge were 'straight out of a war movie'. The distance across the wire was about nine foot. Kelly dived over it and landed on top. When the rest of the men saw him, some thought that this might be part of the plan—to use Kelly as a human bridge. Some started to walk over him. Following a few curses he was helped from the wire and zig-zagged his way up the field.

When he was caught in Holland, he heard the first grenade the Dutch police threw into the flat. He thought it was a bomb and his first thought was 'I'm still alive'. His next thought was 'the SAS have arrived'.

McFarlane was sleeping right under the window. Then a second stun grenade was thrown. Kelly saw a naked body whizz by him. He wasn't too sure who it was. There was a third man in the flat. Kelly thought about the gun in the briefcase at the centre of the room. Suddenly a man appeared and was shouting and screaming at him and holding a shortarm to his face. He realised that he couldn't understand a word the man was saying and it was only then he knew they were Dutch police. The police were shouting about guns and Gerry Kelly had his hands up and was nodding his head from side to side. He was trying to say 'no guns, no guns' with a shortarm belonging to a Dutch policeman shoved into his mouth.

Despite the fact that he has spent since 1973 in prison (with the exception of his period of freedom between 1983 and 1986), he is good humoured and takes a humorous view of how he got caught. At the time of the visit, he was awaiting a verdict on the John Adams charge. If convicted, he would be due to be moved back to the Blocks.

———————————

It was Wednesday 27 April 1988 before the judgment against the escapees was finally handed down—four and a half years after the escape. The Lord Chief Justice of Northern Ireland, Lord Lowry, said that the cause of the death of prison Officer James Ferris had not been proved and sixteen of the eighteen accused were acquitted on the murder charge. The men were sentenced to between three and eight years for their part in the escape. There was surprise. Many of those involved had expected longer sentences.

Harry Murray, the man who had tried to free Billy Gorman from the wire and who was shot running up the field, got eight years for shooting a prison officer in the leg.

———————————

When Billy Gorman jumped out of the back of the lorry he didn't know what to do. He thought the escape was over. He saw some of the men running towards the gate and was surprised to find that nobody made any attempt to stop him. When he got snarled up in the wire, Harry Murray went to help him. Then a prison officer came towards the two of them and ordered the two would-be-escapees to pack it in. An argument developed as to whether the prison officer or Harry Murray should drop the gun.

Billy Gorman put his head down as he knew what was coming next and the prison officer was shot in the leg. Harry took off and Billy Gorman was pulled from the wire.

He was twenty-three at the time. He had been arrested in 1975 and charged with hijacking a van. He got three years probation and in 1977 was given a year for violating that probation. He was charged with killing an RUC man in 1979, an offence which had occurred in 1974 when he was fourteen years old. He was detained at the Secretary of State's pleasure—indefinitely.

Murray had an unusual background for a Provo. He was a Protestant from the Tiger's Bay area of Belfast and had joined the RAF in 1965 as a radar operator. He was dismissed in 1968 for insubordination ('I told my commander to fuck off too often'). He was going out with a Catholic girl and had to leave Tiger's Bay. He married in 1971 and was slowly drawn towards republicanism.

In 1978 he was convicted of the murder of an RUC man in Lisburn and attempted murder of another RUC man in Belfast. He was given two life sentences.

After he was shot, Harry Murray remembers lying on the ground for about fifteen or twenty minutes. A British medical officer pushed past some prison officers that were guarding him to give him attention. He was taken to Lagan Valley Hospital. When he arrived at casualty, the prison officer he had shot was also being treated. Later that night, Murray was being operated on in the city hospital. A doctor asked him if he was allergic to anything. There were two prison officers standing by listening. 'Yeah' he replied, 'screws'.

Lord Lowry sentenced two other leaders for five years each—Brendan McFarlane and Gerry Kelly. As a condition of their extradition from Holland, neither were to be charged with the murder of James Ferris. Kelly was acquitted on the attempted murder of John Adams.

Gerry Kelly had drawn the pistol from his pocket as he approached the Control Room that day. As he had practised often before, he took a two-handed stance with a silver .25. He lowered his head so that when John Adams faced him all

165

the prison officer would see was the top of Kelly's head and the .25. The muzzle of the gun was about two feet away from Adam's face.

The remaining fourteen men were given sentences ranging from three to seven years for imprisoning their guards and possession of weapons. Lord Lowry said that he had considered all the evidence in relation to the death of James Ferris, including that of pathologist Dr Derek Carson. Dr Carson had stated that he could not be certain that his death had been brought about as a result of being stabbed. Lord Lowry said that the cause of death had not been proved. Lord Lowry said that Kelly might well have shot John Adams but the shooting was also attributed to another prisoner and that therefore he could not be satisfied beyond a reasonable doubt. But the Justice was scathing about the evidence given by prison officers in the trial.

He said that it had been impossible to separate 'the wheat from the chaff' in their evidence and this had caused him grave doubt about what they had to say. He said the officers had had 'an unenviable and humiliating experience they would prefer to forget'. He added that an accurate picture of the escape could only come from the prison staff and they had failed to give one.

He said that some officers had given an account of what had happened 'with varying degrees of accuracy'. He said other matters which would reduce his reliance on their evidence was that some of the officers 'may not have been carrying out their duties properly. . . . There is a possibility that not all of them were present at the material time in this high security prison and may have had motives to misdescribe the events to conceal any infractions of their part. They may have had a motive to exaggerate the number of prisoners and the weapons they had used to overpower them.' He also said that many of the officers had contradicted one another and that statements to the RUC had contradicted their written evidence.

Moving on to the escape itself, Lord Lowry said that it had been 'ingeniously planned—cleverly executed' and that it had gone 'amazingly well' until the men reached the Tally Lodge at the main gate. He remarked that the escape was not a 'clandestine flight, but a walk-out, or more accurately, a drive-out in broad daylight under the eyes of a large staff who had access to alarm devices'. The sentences were all to run consecutively for those who were already serving life sentences—about half of the eighteen. For those on determined sentences or on remand at the time of escape, the sentences were to run concurrently.

At the time of writing, Gerry Kelly has just fourteen months left to serve.

If you turn left off the A1 just after it intersects with the M1 on the way to Belfast, you will end up on the Blaris Road, the scene of much confusion among the escapees more than four years ago. After a short while, you will come to the Blocks, nestling snugly in the countryside. First impressions are of wire and corrugated iron. Arriving at visitors' car park, you have to present the visitor's pass to the prison officers on duty. Identification is checked. The routine is much the same as at Crumlin Road Jail.

Everything has to be emptied from the pockets, and a frisk search takes place. From the moment you enter the prison, all dealings with the authorities are done through the name of the prisoner you have come to see. It is almost as if you have no identity outside the prisoner's. This will continue until you retrieve your property at the end of the visit.

You wait in a room with formica chairs and a television. Then there is a journey to the visiting area in a van with no windows. Alsatian dogs can be heard barking behind the corrugated iron fences. Then there is another wait in another room. It doesn't seem to matter whether there are only a few visitors or a few score, it still takes an hour and more to see a prisoner.

Bobby Storey, the OC of the escape, is well over six foot in height. Known to his friends as Big Bob, he is thirty-two and comes from Andersonstown in West Belfast. He is one of a family of four. His involvement, like many of those in H-Blocks, goes back to the early seventies. He was interned on his seventeenth birthday in 1973 and released two years later. He was arrested and charged with blowing up in the Skyway's Hotel at Aldergrove Airport in 1976 and found not guilty the same year. He was re-arrested walking from the court and charged with murder. He was found not guilty in March 1977. He was arrested and charged the same year with the attempted murder of two soldiers during the Queen's visit to Belfast. He was released without ever going to trial on those charges.

He was next arrested in London with Gerry Tuite and Dickie Glenholmes, and charged with conspiring to free Brian Keenan from Brixton prison. He was also charged with conspiracy to cause explosions and possession of weapons. He was found not guilty in a second trial and excluded from England in 1981.

On the day the tenth hunger striker died, 20 August 1981, he was arrested and charged with the attempted murder of a soldier and possession of weapons. He was found guilty of the possession charges and was given eighteen years in June 1982.

He has a forthright and forceful personality and it is easy to see why men were prepared to follow him. Throughout the visit, the prison officers kept a close eye on him. He was one of the four who were caught in the river a short distance from the prison. But for his leadership at the Tally Lodge it's possible that all thirty-eight would have been caught. At a crucial point, he indicated to the prison officers that the men were going to surrender. This calmed things down long enough for the escapees to be able to recompose themselves and make a dash for freedom. The presence and authority of Storey ensured the success of the takeover of H7. He is a major figure within the jail.

One of the men, when asked why he decided to go with Storey, said simply that he had total confidence in him. Prisoners on the inside and the IRA on the outside also had total confidence in Storey. He was known as a man who was able to get things done and make things happen. He would have known what was possible in H7 on the day of the escape and what was not. Following the escape, his name was barely mentioned in the media in connection with leading it. Brendan McFarlane was credited with that. It is fair to say that without Bobby Storey to put Larry Marley's plans into action, there might have been no escape. He is in pretty good humour as he received only seven years for the escape. He was expecting more. Like many others within the Blocks he takes a long-term view of events in the North. In the early seventies five or seven years would have seemed a long time. People thought then that the war would be over in a couple of years. Today five years is a short time.

As a defendant in the escape trial, Bobby Storey was among those who had access to the depositions. These depositions contained statements by prison officers who were expected to give evidence in the trial. Included in those depositions was an exhibit. In this exhibit were two pieces of writing concerning

Storey and Kelly and how they would frighten the lorry driver into doing what they wanted.

According to the writing, Storey was a firm but fair leader and Kelly was a mad bomber and killer who would do anything Storey said. This was the script which was acted out. Both men played their prepared parts out to their satisfaction.

The prison officers would have seen those depositions, and would have learned from the mistakes that were made by their own men. But there was one funny side to the depositions themselves. Included in them were maps and elaborate diagrams of the prison itself. It was ironic that the prisoners had spent months gathering information on the layout of the prison, and the location of key installations, only to be handed them quite openly by the State. Naturally enough, the prison authorities were not pleased that the prisoners should have access to such sensitive information. The only flaw in the argument against giving them the maps was that they already knew every square inch of the prison.

———————

The story of the 1983 escape is ongoing. As each week passes it is possible to add new details. Largely, these new details come to light when an IRA man or woman is killed.

In February 1988, Brendan Burns and Brendan Moley were killed when a bomb they were handling exploded prematurely in County Armagh. Both men had been central to the back-up for the escapees. Brendan Burns was arrested in the South shortly after the escape, and fought extradition back to the North. The authorities wished to charge him with a landmine explosion at Camlough in County Down in May 1981 when five British soldiers were killed. He finally managed to beat all attempts to extradite him back to the North and when he was released he went on the run. He continued to operate in the Armagh area right up until his death.

———————

One of the most enduring memories for many of those that managed to get away was the time most of them met up in the South. The gang that had made the trek down the country and the floorboard men were there. Some hadn't had a drink for years and they arrived at a pub with the intention of having a session which would last a long time. Many of the men on the run played instruments. They started to drink and then Brendan McFarlane picked up a guitar. Seamus Campbell took up the bodhrain. Both men looked across at each other and then McFarlane called 'what'll we play?'

'Can you play *The Sash?*' asked Campbell. McFarlane knew the song well. So did everybody else in the room. And they proceeded to play the anthem of the Orange Order, the song most played on 12 July by loyalist bands. Some of the older republicans present were disgusted that the younger men should behave like that and left. For many of those present the song did not symbolise the Orange State. Rather it was an affirmation that the song belonged as much to republicans as to loyalists.

The session went on through the night and as morning came on people began to leave. It was the last time that the escapees were to come together in such a setting. For one night the war had been far away.

Bibliography

Adams, Gerry, *The Politics of Irish Freedom*, Brandon Press 1986

Asmal, Kadar, *Shoot to Kill?*, Mercier Press 1985

Beresford, David, *Ten Men Dead*, Grafton 1987

Bowyer Bell, J., *The Secret Army*, Sphere 1972

Clarke, A.F.N., *Contact*, Pan 1983

Coogan, Tim Pat, *On the Blanket*, Ward River Press 1970

Devlin, Bernadette, *The Price of My Soul*, Pan 1969

Dillon, Martin, and Lehane, Denis, *Political Murder in Northern Ireland*, Penguin 1973

Farrell, Michael, *Northern Ireland: The Orange State*, Pluto 1980

Farrell, Michael, *Sheltering the Fugitive?*, Mercier Press 1985

Faulkner, Brian, *Memoirs of a Statesman*, Weidenfeld and Nicolson 1978

McGuffin, John, *The Guinea Pigs*, Penguin 1974

Stalker, John, *Stalker*, Harrap 1987

Sunday Times Insight Team, *Ulster*, Penguin 1972

Taylor, Peter, *Beating the Terrorists?*, Penguin 1980

Index